LITTLE CREEK PRESS®
AND BOOK DESIGN

Mineral Point, Wisconsin USA

Little Creek Press® and Book Design
A Division of Kristin Mitchell Design, Inc.
5341 Sunny Ridge Road
Mineral Point, Wisconsin 53565

Editor: Coleman
Book Design and Project Coordination: Little Creek Press

First Edition
October 2017

Printed in Wisconsin, United States of America.

For more information, to contact the author, or to order books:
www.infamousmothers.com

Library of Congress Control Number: 2017954659

ISBN-10: 1-942586-22-1
ISBN-13: 978-1-942586-22-7

Table of Contents

Introduction

by Sagashus T. Levingston

Infamous Mothers is a response to a need. As a graduate student, I took a class on global feminism. It was the first class I had ever taken that was fully dedicated to feminism of any kind. I fell in love with it. Giving me the language and context to understand some of my experiences as a woman, it empowered me. Yet, almost as soon as it made me feel visible, feminism erased me. While the literature and theory gave voice to the struggles of so many women around the world, women from all kinds of backgrounds, I noticed that women like me were absent from this global stage. I am a single mother with six children by four different dads. I am poor... black, and I am an entrepreneur who is also completing a PhD. Where was the voice of women like me in the literature? Equally important, on the pages of articles and books throughout the discipline, where were we imagined as people who made a positive impact in the public sphere? We were either the charity cases people were trying to save or the social pathogens that institutions were trying to correct (and in some case eradicate). Always at one extreme or the other, rarely were we depicted with complexity. Part of the reason for this is that we seldom get to tell our own stories. *Infamous Mothers* is my attempt to address this gap.

In it are the stories of 20 women. All of them are, in one way or another, mothering from the fringes of our society. They were teen mothers, sex workers, drug abusers, or they are single mothers and baby mamas. Some have been abused by men, others abused by their own fears. All of them are black. At the same time, they are women who have lived through circumstances they were never meant to survive. More than this, they are making a difference in our world, today, as doulas, business owners, family advocates, artists, and counselors.

This work is important. It gives complexity and depth to some of the stock stories you hear about black mothers in the media and popular culture. It also provides you with two pieces of the story the news and television dramas rarely give: the narratives of these women's triumphs and the ways in which they matter to our society. The best part is that these women are telling their own stories in their own words using their own voice. Their tales are as eloquent as they are raw. Not only will they challenge everything you thought you knew about an "infamous mother," their testimonies may make you question yourself—and that's not always a bad thing.

To learn more about our work, please visit our website at www.infamousmothers.com. There you will find more information about the makings of this work—including questions and answers about the target audience, methods, challenges, and so on. You will find additional study guides and resources. You can get details about our programming, speaking engagements, and Infamous Mothers memberships. You can also submit questions to us via Live Chat or by sending us a message by clicking Contact. I look forward to connecting with you. ❊

Acknowledgements

On my own, I am limited. But with you, I can do anything. So many people have contributed to both the creation of me and my work. I am, as I heard a woman once say, "the product of 10,000 hands."

The first set of hands I'd like to thank comes from throughout the University of Wisconsin-Madison. I am so proud of the training I received from the Departments of Afro-American Studies and English. Thank you for the exposure, the theory, the support. I am especially thankful for my dissertation committee—Cherene Sherrard-Johnson, Michael Bernard-Donals, Aida Levy-Hussen, and Craig Werner. Thank you Susan Stanford Friedman, Tejumola Olaniyan, and Leslie Bow for exposing me to my first classes and/or readings on feminism. Finally, I thank the staff and leadership of Eagle Heights and the Office of Childcare and Family Resources. You made it possible for me to live while I pursued my dream.

I'd like to thank all of the Kickstarter supporters that made this project possible. In July of 2016, 253 people came together and pledged $25,617 to help us make the *Infamous Mothers* prototype. We had a blast! While I especially want to thank Kamal and Christin-Gates Calloway for getting us to our goal, everyone's contribution made all the difference. Thank you.

I want to send all my love to the YWCA-Madison, the Catalyst Project, and DAIS. To the organizations, thank you for trusting me with your clients. Thank you for allowing me to work with them on a regular basis. Thank you for creating a space for this work. Thank you for

allowing me to experience, over and over again, the reality that this matters. It makes a difference. Thank you for allowing me to share the stories in this book and pilot the curriculum with your residents and/or staff. I will forever appreciate your choice to try me when no one even knew my name. Thank you.

While this *Infamous Mothers* book project is my brainchild, amazing collaborators made it come alive. Coleman, there is no way I could've edited those stories and produced what you did. Without fail, you were able to identify the heart of each narrative. Whether the task before you was 500 pages of transcript or 30 pages, you got it right every time. Kristin could not have chosen a better person for this job. Thank you.

Tanisha Pyron, you stepped into the vision of this work, and without missing a beat, captured extraordinary images. As the assistant photographer, you were able to produce work that connected seamlessly with the lead shooter's. As a sister, friend, and brand ambassador, you shared our work across all your platforms, listened to my ideas and encouraged me constantly. Your eloquence gave voice to my ideas at times when I fumbled the most with them. Thank you. Thank you for getting on the road and driving across states for photo shoots and for showing up in Chicago for a sister circle when I couldn't. Thank you for, when you were flailing and floundering in the reality of your own life, showing up for me when it seemed no one was there for you. I see you. And I thank you. I thank you for your many prayers, your patience, and your kind words.

Damian Pearson, you have been my bestest bestie since the third grade. You are my secret keeper, the godfather, my biggest advocate, and my mirror. Thank you for ALWAYS supporting me—especially now.

Dr. Amy Gannon, life is so much more fun because we get to walk this earth together. There is no coach like you. So much of my life has been about cutting off pieces of myself to fit into a box. And then I met you, and you allowed me to bring my whole self to my work. You allowed me to be a mother, an entrepreneur, and an academic. You never made me choose. That is a rare thing. Thank you. Thank you for all the laughs, the goofy faces, the memes, the hard work. Thank you for role modeling for me what it means to live a genuine and authentic life. And thank you for being the co-founder of the women's organization that made *Infamous Mothers* a reality. This work is growing because, week after week, you helped me build a foundation that was unique, true to my vision, and sustainable. You are badass.

My extended family is amazing. My aunts, uncles, cousins, nieces, and nephews have spent countless hours supporting me in all the ways they know how. Each one of you have bragged on me, praised me, watched a kid (or three), braided hair, given an encouraging word, cleaned out my car, driven some child (or two) across states, prayed for me, listened, wired money, shown up to events... loved me. In the day-to-day of making this all happen, it's so easy to forget that all of you have loved and supported me. And it has all counted. Thank you.

With my mother, father, and brother and sister-in-law, I have traveled a rocky road filled with arguments and fallouts. But the bottom line has always been love. All of you have shown up, sacrificed, protected, guided, supported, and loved me. You have given me advice and had hard conversations with me. I am strong because of you. You have done so much to make sure I could make it. Thank you for your accountability, your dollars, your late-night conversations. Ma, thank you for always being available to listen to me. And, when I got old enough, thank you for making life less about me and more about you. You deserve it. Thank you for being so funny and down to earth. I always say, other folks could've been my mom. But I am so glad I got you. Ike (dad), thank you for giving me my name and for teaching me what it means. Bobby, thank you for being my biggest protector and for always fighting for me. Toni, thank you for keeping your word from the conversation we had a long time ago.

Tosumba, you are the boy version of me. Some of the childhood traumas I've had to overcome, you are working to overcome. I have a thousand children; you have a thousand. I have control issues; you have control issues. Yet, we manage to still stick this thing out because we both know something beautiful just might be on the other side. Thank you for finding the strength to stay when no one else could.

Dianna, Yemi, Cho, Ryland, Brooklyn, and Layden—thank you. I am so flawed. But you choose to love and follow me and allow me to mother you, despite my shortcomings. You have trusted me with your lives. Each of you have sacrificed for our larger vision of family and community. You have been so proud of me and my work even while you walked around with holes in your shoes or slept on pallets on the floor. Because each of you exist, I was able to finally dream. You all inspire my work—and you inspire me. I am so proud of each and every one of you. And I am thankful that you have allowed me to grow up with you. ❋

❃

We are teen moms, single mothers,

mothers who once sex worked and were addicted to crack.

We're not your average good girls.

We are survivors of domestic abuse, sexual trauma.

But we're not your damsels in distress.

We are women with moxie and grit.

We are game changers and powerhouses.

We are women who have not only been to the belly of hell and survived,

we are mothers who managed to bring something good back.

We came out on the other side

as attorneys, doctors, artists, nurse practitioners, homeowners, counselors,

and so much more.

We are 20 mothers who make a difference in this world.

Read our stories and witness how.

❃

Tanisha

I was a teenage mother. I got pregnant while I was still in high school, but I successfully finished. I also have connections to the adult entertainment industry. I worked for four years as a stripper shortly after I gave birth to my son. It was the first job that I got, but in truth, it was a job I sought out for many reasons, primarily because it fit perfectly into every insecurity and all the negative messages I had received over the course of my life about my beauty, my body, and my sexuality. And the money was good, sometimes even great, and I needed money.

Part of me was rebelling through being a teen mother, through sex, and yet, another part of me was doing exactly what I was programmed to do. I remember it being a huge deal in my family because good girls, smart girls, girls who lead school assemblies and make the honor roll DON'T get pregnant in high school, though the men and boys in my family kinda did whatever they wanted. Case in point, shortly after I found out I was pregnant, a male cousin got two women pregnant at the same time. Even my own father, who had two long-term domestic partnerships, five children and waited 22 long years to marry my stepmother, was shaking his head. The males in my family had a freedom not afforded to the women and girls. I felt like I had let my father down, like I had let my whole family down.

I was raised with a really sweet mother and a traditional black, macho father. My womanhood bounced off

their energy like a pinball my entire life. I didn't have a lot of affirmation outside of what my dad did or did not approve. There are other contributing factors that I can share, but it's my story, and I really don't want to make it about my mom or my dad. There are parts of their lives I wouldn't be comfortable with sharing. But what I will say is that there was definitely trauma.

I grew up poor, like a lot of black folks. My parents split when I was nine. By then, I had experienced molestation, verbal and emotional abuse, and toxic dynamics via caregivers, friends of the family, and community members. By the time I had my son and was dancing in the clubs, there were a series of events that led up to it.

My freshman year, my mother and my father ended up in custody court, and my dad won custody of us from my mother. That probably was the biggest reason why I ended up a teen mom. There was just very little protection for my womanhood and really very little guidance, but a lot of male expectations of womanhood and beauty in general.

And being a dark-skinned woman, I remember a lot of years in my life, my teenager years in particular, when the only thing that people seemed to be affirming was that I was really smart and that I was sexy. Nobody ever called me pretty. I was one of those girls that the boys ignored in school. I was gangly, long-limbed, awkward, and had thick glasses. I was dark. But the boys would call on the phone later. I was about 14 or 15 when that started.

And then you mix trauma with that. You mix not seeing my mother on a day-to-day basis for two-and-a-half years and it being an extreme situation. There were a couple summers where I wasn't protected at all, and those are the summers when my body started to develop, when the niggas started ride through the neighborhood real slow talking about, "Do you need a ride home?" knowing damn well you're 15.

There was a summer where I was just hurting, and there was always some guy there to take advantage of

slave plantation metaphor, we would call it "the moment that you break." You hear it in the conversation of pimps today, the idea of breaking a bitch or breaking a woman.

I ended up leaving my dad's house because of his temperament and his views on women. I ended up getting in my car one day, at about 16, and driving to my mama's house in Saginaw. When I got there, she wasn't really in a place to receive me. I hopped from couch to couch, and a girlfriend's mom let me stay for a bit. But I didn't have anywhere to go. I ended up meeting a man who was about ten years older than me, and he took

...it was a job I sought out for many reasons, primarily because it fit perfectly into every insecurity and all the negative messages I had received over the course of my life about my beauty, my body and my sexuality, and the money **was good, sometimes even great, and I needed money.**

those moments, to exploit and capitalize on my weakness and vulnerability, sort of compounding the issues I already had. I began to doubt my own worth. The only thing anybody ever affirmed was that I was sexy. Nobody ever said "pretty." They never said "beautiful." They just said "sexy." I could see my innocence erode over time. That continual vulnerability and predatory thing, I know intimately. I KNOW how many times that walk home from school happens before you end up in the back seat of a guy's car or before you end up at a hotel underage. My experience as a young woman of color I liken to the experiences of a young man of color who is walking to and from school every day past gang members and drug dealing. There is a corrosive enticement to compromise, and over time, you find yourself weakening. Using a

me in, underage, to "help" me, but what he really was doing was fucking my young ass and kicking my young ass, that's what he was doing.

I didn't then and don't know now what the edges of my womanhood are. I still surprise myself and don't know what I'm capable of completely. As a woman, I'm still expanding and growing. As a teenager, I wasn't able to articulate that about myself. I felt like a grown-up playing house with this man, had no idea what it was to be a grown-up at all. And as soon as I took that pregnancy test, I just knew that I couldn't stay there, that he was too toxic and too violent and either he was going to kill me or I was going to kill him. I knew this man could pop me upside my head one day, and instead of me balling up, I could break one of those lamps over his head and go to jail. So we had to separate. Or he'd break a lamp over my head, and I wouldn't wake up. So we had to separate, and I went from him sexualizing me to the world doing it in clubs.

After I left my son's father, I ended up moving back to my hometown, and a cousin let me stay with her for a little bit, but I knew that wasn't going to work. By the time I had my son, I remember how hard it was just trying to live, survive, and be a good woman. That's a theme in my mothering, the cost of trying to be a good woman while surviving.

I was pregnant and walking over an overpass every single day two miles to and from work because the bus didn't go to the Meijer's that I worked at. And it did have a negative effect on my pregnancy. I ended up going into preterm labor because of the workload. Oh my goodness, I'm going to cry. The workload was hard and heavy and a burden, and I was alone as a teen dealing with it.

Because of all of the walking and just not having anybody to protect me or care about me, my placenta abrupted. My water broke at 27 weeks. I almost died. My baby almost died. And three weeks later, they were trying to keep me from going into labor too soon. My baby came out. He was due late January, and I had my baby

November 8. He spent the whole winter in the hospital. He was two pounds 4.5 ounces when I had him, and 14 inches long.

I remember there was a girl from my high school who I had heard was a stripper in Flint, Michigan. And I remember thinking, "If she can be a stripper and make money and get on, hey, maybe I can." And I went and did an amateur night, and it's so strange to me now how strippers and stripping is sort of idolized.

People ask me what it was like. Was it sexy, or thrilling, or fun, or adventurous? My answer is always the same: it was like being naked in a room full of strangers. Butt-bare naked, new-baby body, new-mommy pooch, in a room full of strangers. I think I even wore the little pumps that I wore to my junior prom. I didn't even have stripper shoes. I had some bras that I got from Kmart. I didn't have any of the right stuff, but once it started, the money came quickly.

The hustle came naturally to me because I was a smart girl, and prior to getting pregnant, I was doing well in school. I am the first child in my family and have always been a traditional, archetypal achiever. I had won awards for numerous things including public speaking. And I went to national public speaking competitions, played sports, started clubs, and gave the black history speeches. I was that girl in school.

My ability to talk to people and my intelligence helped me thrive as a dancer. I took my intelligence with me into that darkness, and I adapted it in the hustle. But it was a continually sexualizing environment. It was like being Tweety Bird in a room full of Sylvester the Cats. It was brutal in a lot of regards.

I didn't go through stuff that a lot of other girls went through because I got into a relationship with an ex of mine as soon as I got my own place. The young man had

a similar life story as my own. We had a great friendship, and we just seemed to gravitate to one another and ended up in a five-year relationship.

The whole time I was a stripper, I was in a relationship. I always had a home to go to. I had a man who would drop me off at work and pick me up, and not in a pimp-mobile. He worked two jobs, menial jobs at times, jobs that other men I've dated would never take. He worked at Subway, and he worked at a lab keeping up rats, like discarding rats or something. I had a little family, so that was my experience while I was in the sex industry. I had this whole other life where the part of me that had been the most abused was celebrated, in a perverse sense. And I think that's really the heart of the infamy, and the success. Oh, my goodness, I'm going to cry again!

That part of me is what God is actually redeeming in my art—that I am sexy but not sexualized by others. And I can offer and speak my truth and be beautiful and be captivating but also have sexuality in my artwork—the pain, the real pain and the real trauma of real complexities connected to my type of black womanhood.

I don't think that you get to a place where you make yourself a subversive black girl without going through some stuff that requires you to be an antihero in your narrative and go against the grain. It is essential to your survival as a woman of color. The things that I went through now require me to be a rigorous advocate for myself, that I stand up. It's like you can only be molested so much, and abused, and raped, and put down, and constantly inappropriately touched, even in a verbal sense, before you finally say, "Okay, stop. That's enough."

I believe there's a little bit of my soul, my journey, and struggle in a whole lot of women. It's makes me able to identify, empathize, not judge, show up for, or give the kind of words that I needed when I was walking that mile-and-a-half to Meijer's.

I had to find balance for myself, and a lot of that has been my connection to Christ and getting saved and having a relationship with Him, not necessarily the church. That's another part of the story. The black church further traumatized me around my body and my sexuality, as I found myself in the familiar place of working to be good enough to be a good woman, a recycled virgin, clean enough for some sensible deacon to wanna marry.

My superpower is my intuition. The Bible talks about how Jesus would enter a room and he would read the hearts of the men in the room, and he didn't trust himself with them. And I think that the discernment, that Holy Spirit discernment that I have, that is the thing that kept me from getting in the wrong car when I was dancing. That's the thing that kept me from ingesting too much of the toxicity the world tried to saturate me in. Racial stuff. Things around color and skin tone and who can be pretty. The thing that kept me from all of that was my intuition, and my ability to look at someone and say, "There's something going on with that person. You don't have to go there and talk to them. That's not going to be good for you." So that was and is my superpower—discerning the hearts of men.

My story is one that is still unfolding. I would say the most beautiful part, or the part of my mothering experience that I'm most excited about, is in front of me. I'm excited about what's happening with my son. There's some-

thing divine about that. I have invested so much into this young man. And to see him tall, strong, intelligent, goal-oriented, hopeful about his life—you know, sort of transitioning into independent living—he is my greatest success. He is my greatest legacy, in addition to the art and people that I've touched.

It has taken me a lifetime to differentiate between the woman that I am and the programming that came from others. It has taken me a lifetime to be able to understand my sexuality as something different from the whore the world wanted to make me out to be. My art reflects that. It is about bringing balance to young women like me. Maybe their parents are in a state to help them understand things, maybe not. But I want my art to help women understand that your identity is more than who you are on your most vulnerable and worst day.

In my whole life as a brown girl, I felt like the whole world was trying to get me to conform to something that I am inherently not. From my hair, to the press and comb, to the perms, to weaves, to wigs, trying to get my hair to be something that it's not. Trying to get my skin tone, my eye color, everything should be something different than what it is. I need to be less mouthy, because girls aren't supposed to be as mouthy as I was with my father, or as intelligent and a critical thinker as I am now.

It is okay, it is more than fair and right, it is a divine thing to just be you. That's the thing that made the tumblers start to fall into place for me. That I am enough. ✿

Angela

I had my first son one month before my 18th birthday. I had another one three years after that, and another one three years after that, and a daughter three years after that. All of my children are three years apart. My oldest is now 25. My next one is 22. I have a 19-year-old and a 16-year-old.

My parents didn't find out until my eighth month that I was pregnant because I was the typical teenager. I'd come home and I'd go in my room. You know, walk right past them. "You want to watch a movie with us?" "No, I'm okay." I'd go in my room and I'd hide it.

One day my mom was in the kitchen talking on the phone to her sister—her normal routine—and I was hungry. As I opened the refrigerator, she got a side glance of me. By that time, my clothes were getting tight. The sweater I had on revealed my bump. She saw it, and that's when we had that talk.

The guy I was pregnant by had already cheated on me twice—just to be real—and I didn't know how to tell them that. To my surprise, my parents were very understanding. I didn't expect that at all. I was humiliated, scared, and most of all, I didn't want to disappoint them.

When I wanted to quit, my mother was right there. I had my grandmother talking to me like "this is not the end for you." My dad instilled in us, my two brothers and me, the importance of working. We spent countless hours doing everything from yard work to washing walls. They didn't enable me. They were just like "this is not the end."

They didn't allow me to lay in a bed of depression. I had to get up and do what I needed to do.

At first I decided I wanted to do hair, be a beautician. I enrolled in school, decided that wasn't for me. Then I went on to be a CNA, passed the state certification and wasn't fulfilled. I didn't plan on being a child care provider or in a daycare center. It happened that way. I took my children to a daycare center I couldn't afford. I applied for assistance to no avail. The intake worker suggested that I work days and my husband work nights if we couldn't afford to send our children to child care. The bill got too high, so I ended up moving them to a home daycare. When I got to the home daycare, I saw things that I didn't like. That's when I decided that I would open my own daycare and care for my own kids. (At that time, I had three children and one was on the way. The makings of a mini-camp was already in the process.) I enrolled at MATC and took the introductory class to child care courses.

Shortly after that, I became certified through the state of Wisconsin and started an in-home daycare. My waiting list kept growing and growing by word of mouth. Not by advertising on social media, like Facebook, Instagram etc. None of that. It was all word of mouth from what parents saw.

I decided that I was going to go out and find a place to open a child care center. I'm like, "Ma,"—because my mom was my backbone—"help me find this place." (My parents moved to Madison to support me when they found out that I was getting a divorce. Their house sold in three days, and they were here within the month.) We started looking online at different places and talking to realtors.

The child care center I am currently in used to be St. Vincent de Paul. I remember looking through the window and writing down the guy's phone number. "How much is this place?" I asked. He threw these huge numbers out there. In my mind, I was like, "Oh, no, no, no, no, no, I can't afford that." So then I called him again 30 days later. "I see that the building is still for lease. How much is it?" He threw these long numbers out there again, so I thanked him for his time.

One month later I called back again. I said, "Hey, Larry, it's Angela." By that time we were on a first-name basis. He asked if I had a business plan. I told him yes. Then he asked me if I had a budget. I told him I did. We set up a meeting. I had a whole portfolio of photos from when I first started caring for children. I had reference letters. I then presented him with my waiting list. He asked why I wanted to do child care. I told him my grandma would care for me and my cousins every year for summer vacations. There would be at least 15 of us. We would sleep seven to a bed, some on the couch and some would sleep on pallets (a bunch of covers on the floor). I continued to tell him those were the best experiences of life. We cooked together; we told scary stories; we made up silly games that I plead the Fifth on to this

very day. We disagreed; we laughed; we loved; but most important, we were allowed to be children.

"Well, can you afford this amount?" he asked. Again, it was extremely high. "No, it's out of my range." "Can you afford this?" "No, still too high." His next question was: "Well, how much can you afford?" I told him. He said, "Okay." By the grace of God, he saw something in me and decided to support my dream. During the next two years, I remodeled the building by having sliding doors installed in two rooms, a bathroom installed with multiple toilets and sinks, Plexiglas windows, and had the kitchen remodeled. I felt that if he could put that faith in me, I could do the same thing for him. My dream was coming to life!

People look at me and don't see what I've been through. The struggle is very real.

Everything hasn't always been good. My lights and heat have been disconnected multiple times. As a child, I remember my family walking to the bus stop in the middle of the night in the dead of winter, freezing, to take the bus to a friend's house to take baths because our heat was off. I also remember my daddy boiling water on the stove so we could have a hot bath. That's why I'm humble and keep doing what I'm doing, because I've been in difficult situations and can relate to what others go through.

Do I get tired? Yes, yes! I learned over the years that I have to give it to God. Give it to God. Take one day at a time, and give it to God. And that's what I do. There were so many days where I just felt like giving up. Coming into a new business with no grants, no funding, no donations. Just a dream of making a difference in someone's life. You know? Even now, no grants, no funding, no donations. It's all me.

People don't understand where we come from as black people. They don't know how to read in between the lines. Some see us as angry. No, he's not angry, he's struggling because he can't find a job, or she has to wear the same pair of pants with a different shirt three days out of the week. Or she must be on public assistance getting food stamps. I remember someone making a comment about their taxes going to pay for my kids. At that time, I was working a full-time job, and I wasn't getting assistance. People just assume all sorts of things when you're a young parent. I now understand why my dad would come home in silence. Having to work twice as hard though equally educated, watching others get promoted to jobs he was overqualified for, trying to sustain a suitable job in a harsh environment while taking care of his family. How do you balance life in a system that's made to keep you down?

My husband and I were having a lot of ups and downs in 2006. I didn't want my daughter to think that it was okay to be treated in negative ways, and I didn't want my sons to think that it was okay to hit or talk down to a woman. In 2008, when the divorce was final, it was a difficult time for us, including my ex. He went through a depression stage where he just stopped—everything. Stopped calling, stopped coming by, stopped going to the parent-teacher conferences. He stopped everything. You couldn't have paid me to believe he would do that. Not the man "who always held it down"—my grandmother's words. Not the man who spent countless nights helping with homework and spending time with his children.

I had to keep moving forward even though my children were falling apart, literally. Heck, to be honest, I was, too. We were both supposed to tell the kids about the divorce at the same time. At the last minute, he decided that he didn't want to tell them. So he left me alone to explain to the kids why mommy and daddy weren't going to be together anymore.

I see posts on Facebook where women are talking about I'm the mama and the daddy. (Side note: There are a lot of fathers who are not given props where props are due.) I was wise enough to know that I couldn't be the daddy, but at the same time, I was in the position where I had to be. I had to be Mama and I had to take up some of the slack and be Daddy, and I had to put on the happy face at church. Then I had to come to work smiling, like "Hi, everything is okay!" And my whole world was falling apart.

Have you ever been in a situation where your kitchen cabinets are full, your refrigerator is full, but there's nothing that you want to eat because you have catered to everyone in your house except you? I had been taking care of everyone so long that I didn't know how to take care of myself. I'm just getting to the point where I'm learning to take care of me.

I had learned not to cry when I wanted to cry. Sometimes life does not allow you to stand still, to care for yourself. I had to pick up the pieces. My little ones were depending on me. I can remember times within those years where I had so many different emotions built up inside of me that I would go in the closet, close the door, hold a pillow to my face, and just scream.

There's a Scripture that says in order to be forgiven, you must forgive. I had so much anger in my heart that I'm like, "God, please don't take me out; don't let me die until I forgive, because I need to be forgiven for all the stuff that I've done wrong." I know I'm not a saint.

It's funny how your children will remind you of things you taught them. Train up a child in the way they should go, and they will not depart from it. I remember venting to my oldest son, who at that time was attending a parent-teacher conference on my behalf because I had to be at his brother's concert, saying to me "You know you have to forgive, right?" I wanted to ask: boy who in the world taught you that?!! Eventually, I forgave.

A lot of people drink and do drugs because they don't want to face reality. I had to stop myself from going down that road. There were times I was like, man, I just need a drink. I need to go somewhere by myself and sit down and unwind. And then I said, this can't be my every day.

I had low self-esteem growing up. My older brother used to always call me ugly. "Ugly, get away from me. Ugly this. Ooh, that's ugly." So everything I did was ugly, including me—I was ugly. I remember him in the bathroom with my mom asking, "Why your friends' kids are cute and Angela's so ugly?" It wasn't until my high school years that I started to realize I was fine! And big butts were hot! I was like heyyy now! You know, light skin was in at that time, too. I remember Spike Lee's movie School Daze had just came out. E.U. has a song on the sound track called "Doing Da Butt." Whenever I heard, "Angela got a big old butt," I was like, "Oh yeah!" As corny as it may sound, that made me feel proud of who I was.

For this very reason, family meetings were started in our home. Rules were set: 1. Anyone could call a meeting, no matter the age. 2. Everyone's feelings are to be considered and their opinion counts. 3. We don't call names, and we don't make fun of each other. Enough of that goes on outside of these walls. Home is where the heart is. 4. Whatever goes on in this meeting stays in this meeting. If you have something you need to say, then you can say it. 5. Make a conscious effort to make a change.

an who appears to have it all. I'm not really picky about what a man has, but respect is huge for me. He must smell good and wear a watch and his shoes, his shoes tell me who he is. I've dated people whose income is lower than mine, and I've dated men whose income is three times higher than mine. I don't date men for what they have; I date them for their heart, who they are inside. We could eat a pizza, eat steak at a five-star restaurant, go to the opera, watch a movie or just chill. That could be our date, and I'm happy as long as we have a good conversation going and good vibes.

My superpower is changing armor. It's a unique type of armor that's capable of changing from one form to another. It could be either used as a tool or a weapon.

Do I get tired? Yes, yes! I learned over the years that I have to give it to God. Give it to God. Take one day at a time, and give it to God. And that's what I do. There were so many days where I just felt like giving up.

It's so important to build each other up. I tell my children to find something about themselves that they love and flaunt it. That's also my advice to every woman or man. Find something about yourself and love it, because it's something that you have that some someone else wish they had. I find myself staring at others' hands sometimes, wishing my skin was smooth. I have what seems to be the hands of an 80-year-old because my skin dries out from eczema. I feel like everyone has something about herself that's beautiful or unique.

Fast forward to 2016. It's hard to date because I think I intimidate men. Some men are afraid to approach a wom-

As your armor changes, it kind of protects you from damage.

Don't let the haters influence what you've got going on. If you believe that you can do it, go for it.

Twenty-five years later, I remain humble. Remembering the 17-year-old, pregnant, unwed, scared, looked-down-on, talked-about, raised-in-the-inner-city of Chicago girl whose life has changed for the better because she decided to defy the odds and the myths. Not fully who I will become but well on my way. There's triumph in my tragedy. ❖

Jennifer

When I had my last kid in 2011, I started going to school at Olive-Harvey City College of Chicago, where I work. When I transferred to National Louis University a couple of years later, I had pretty much obtained maybe 80 percent of the courses I needed to get the associate's degree. But my goal was a bachelor's—period.

I waited until I took the math credit for National Louis, because I needed it for the bachelor's, too. And when I passed it, I was able to send my transcript from Olive-Harvey for the associate's, and that's how I ended up getting both degrees in the same year.

I have four kids and a grandchild: a son, 15, a son, 11, a girl, 5, and my daughter is 18 who has a baby. The conversations in this house are about graduating, about education. If I can do it, I cannot accept any excuse from them why they can't.

I'm working full-time, in school full-time, raising my kids full-time. And it has not been easy. It's been a collaborative effort. Like my mom, if it wasn't for her, I'm almost certain I would have given up. Mom would come over, cook some dinner, try to alleviate a job that I would have to do.

My kids have all stepped up and assisted. My oldest son is a really good typist because I had to have him help me type discussion posts while I'm working on another one. I had to teach him, you know, APA citations and all kinds of stuff.

I've wanted to quit. I'd say, "You know what, I'll wait till the kids are a little older." But there is no "wait" at this point anymore.

Accomplishing things makes me feel like I'm repaying myself in some way.

I was trying to get some more money at work. Once I started seeing I could really do this, I wanted more. I wanted more, and I just wanted my kids to see that regardless of me having a baby at 17 and another one at 19, that didn't make me give up, though I've wanted to—many, many a time. But it's just... it's just a will to fight and get through.

I had a really bad breakup with my youngest child's dad about three years ago, and it was just very shocking and hurtful. That was like the final straw of a man disrespecting me.

And it almost took me out. I felt very suicidal and it scared me, because I've never felt that low. I lost a lot of weight. My mom was worried about me, the kids were worried about me. And then I'd say, you know what? Nobody's going to help you. You've got to help yourself. And I decided to seek therapy.

A lot of things that I had never spoken of before I was able to finally let out. And I think that is what got me to a point where I could address some of my internal thoughts like, you know, this is... well, this is why you didn't get married, this is why you settled for this, this is why you think you're not worthy of X, Y, and Z.

And so, from that point the negative thoughts just kind of released, changed.

I had to address things head-on, like being molested as a child. I knew it was going to be rough, and I knew it was going to be hard, but I had to do it because I was at rock bottom. I'd been pushing it down for years and years and then it started blowing up in my face.

Well, that was like my turning point, I'd say.

I couldn't control my emotions. I was angry. I was mad. I felt like I just had lost all control of my life. And it was just blowing up in my face and there was nothing I could do about it.

But the therapy helped me to say "you do have control."

welfare mother (which I don't see anything wrong with).

I was still a kid myself. I had a lot of growing up to do. When my daughter was young, my mom would get her and I'd be out in the street, you know, playing about. I had a baby in childhood.

People had written me off. I see people now that haven't seen me in years. They're completely surprised and shocked that I have a degree, or I work in a decent job and have a house when people didn't think I would amount to anything.

When my daughter had the baby, we were already tight. Four kids and a mom in a two-bedroom apartment. When she had the baby, that's another child I had to get in the apartment. And I felt like okay, I'm definitely

Accomplishing things makes me feel like I'm repaying myself in some way.

I was giving so many different people control over my own happiness. You know what I'm saying? Like oh, this man doesn't want me. That must mean that I'm nothing. I'm not worthy.

Recognizing how somebody treated me is not a reflection of me but a reflection of who they are—it took a while to get that point. And it's still something I struggle with. It's not like I'm 100 percent healed.

I had to change the voices in my head to say, "I deserve this. I'm worthy of this."

I had a child at 17, then turned around two years later and had another child and with a different father.

Many people, many people did not think that I would amount to anything—you know, be a statistic,

going to have to move and probably get a three-bedroom or try to rent a house.

When people tell me, "black people don't help each other"—that is not true. That is not true. I was helped by people. And my brother (not biological but brother as in he was a black man), he was a realtor, young guy, not too much older than me. I'm like: "Look, I've got four kids. I can't afford to pay a whole lot more than I'm paying in rent for a house."

I finally found this house, and at the end of the day, I got it. I'm paying $80 more than I did in a two-bedroom. That included the mortgage, the homeowner's insurance, and the mortgage tax. And that was a blessing. God is working through people to help me.

I got a bachelor of science in management. The associate degree is in general studies.

I want what I've experienced and what I've been able to accomplish to inspire other young black women. Women, period, but definitely my people. And in my role at work, at Olive-Harvey College, I am in contact with young sisters.

What's going to be the best way that I can help others, especially my people—that's what I'm attuned to. What can I do?

What kind of career can I make in my graduate program? I'm thinking of going into public policy, because I feel like that's where the change is going to start. We've got to start changing these policies and changing these "no, you can't..."

My superpower is perseverance.

Regardless of the situation, regardless of what I've been through, I've been able to persevere.

When I was dealing with the breakup of a seven-year relationship and then not even a few months later my daughter giving birth, that was a moment when I had to persevere. And I was still in school, mind you, when all of this was happening. But then I said, "You know what, I'm going to be honest with my professors." And I was.

I emailed them and told them I have some personal issues going on. I even told them my daughter has a baby. And my assignments are going to be late, and I just want the opportunity to turn them in even if I'm going to lose credit.

My professors cared. My reputation as a student was enough that they knew that I'm not the type to just turn in late assignments. I'm not the type to make up something to get out of turning in stuff.

That really gave me a lot of strength, to be honest, and that's when I knew "I'm going to get through this." ✽

Carol

I am an infamous mother. I have two children. My older child's name is Bobby, like his father. I had my son at the age of 20. And my daughter's name is Sagashus.

I was a virgin at 19. The first time I had sex, I got pregnant. So I had to get married. I got married because of stigma, not because of love. I shouldn't of got married, but back then, in the 60s, people looked down on you if you were a single mom.

I got married because I was afraid that people would judge me. That made me not like my son. I blamed him, since the first time I had sex, he decided he wanted to come. I was ignorant. I wasn't a lovable mother towards my boy. I was abusive. Verbally, I was very abusive.

When he was small, he was a nice little kid. He never gave me a hard way to go, not knowing that I didn't really like him. But as he got older, he started getting in trouble. He was in and out of jail during his teenage days and his young adult life.

I was one of those people, everything was centered around me; it was all about me. I was frustrated and angry and depressed because my dream was gone—my dream of becoming someone great.

Bobby's father loved him. Also, his father was one of those men that cared for his family financially, so he didn't want me to work or go to school. That was a problem with me because I was still wanting to go to school and have a career.

My husband, he loved me, but I wasn't in love with him, not in the beginning. (I grew to love him later in our marriage.) When he was at work, instead of me just staying at home, cooking and cleaning, I would sneak out and take classes to learn about the computer. Because they said that was going to be the big thing, computers, I wanted to learn all about them. Back then, typing was a big deal. If you knew how to do that, you were in demand. But they said eventually the computer was going to take over. I believed them, so I pursued that. Doing so meant, at times, I wasn't around Bobby. I had to get babysitters, and he would cry all the time. He never wanted to go to the babysitter.

I started college at the age of 17. I received my bachelor's degree at the age of 42. I went to college for 25 years. At this point in my life, Bobby's father and I had broken up. That left me on my own. I had my own apartment; I had a roommate.

I was experimenting with sex and enjoying me. I was out partying. I worked at Playboy in the deli department. Tips helped me pay for my tuition.

So I'm still going to school, Bobby and I have moved out and we have our own apartment, but I'm still not there for him. His father eventually came and got him, and he spent his teenage days with his father in a place where he didn't want to be. He wanted to be with me. I'm out here enjoying my life now, with the sex and being around people that were into drugs, although I wasn't into drugs.

Meantime, I met my present husband. I'm mature now. By the time I met him, I'm in my late 20s. He and I both decided we wanted to have a child. Now I'm ready to have a child. I didn't want to love the new one more than I loved the old one, and I didn't want any jealousy going on. For some reason, being pregnant with the new child made me enjoy my older son. With this new child that was coming, I didn't want to make the same mistakes that I made with Bobby.

It turned out that the child was a girl, Sagashus. I had her during a point in my life when I was happy. By the time she came, I knew who I was. I was still going to school. My confidence was up. I was beginning to get Cs and some Bs.

When I birthed my son, I was numbed with pain. I was screaming; I was howling. The nurses didn't want to come around me. I was just hell. When I had this daughter, I didn't have no pain. It was a beautiful pregnancy. When I went into labor, I didn't even know. My husband and I were having sex, and he said, "Carol, I think you getting ready to have a baby." I said, "I can't be ready to have a baby, ain't nothing busted." He said, "I think you better go to the hospital anyway."

When the doctor examined me, he said, "Oh yeah, you getting ready to have a baby!" They burst the water. I said, "Baby's on its way out, and I have no pain? I ain't never heard of this before in my life."

Sagashus' head was so huge that she couldn't come out through the canal without help. I'm still not having any pain, but when her father saw that they put those tongs up in me, he fainted. I'm still saying, "Where's the pain?"

Sagashus came out, and she was a very little baby, only six pounds. She came out with her eyes open. The doctors looked at her and they said, "This baby's going to be something great!" I'm saying to myself, "This baby's only five minutes old. How in the world can you judge this?"

They took this baby to some room and did all kinds of examinations. They came back, and they said, "This baby is a genius." I'm saying to myself how in the world can they know? I explained this kid is not gonna be all you're talking about because I live in a ghetto, and in a ghetto geniuses do not bloom and survive.

When I took the baby home, the baby was three days old. My sister lived with me, and she said to me, "Carol, that baby is three days old and that baby is moving." She wasn't crawling, but she was scooting around. We said, "Wait a minute, we've never seen a three-day baby scooting around."

I'm still going to school, and now I have Sagashus and Bobby. He's 14-years-old. Bobby saw me and this new baby—all this love and affection—and he remembered he didn't get that from me. That made him jealous. He was hating on this little baby.

Now five years have passed. I'm in my 40s now, and I'm still going to school. Sagashus started kindergarten, and she was smarter than I was in college. I used to tell her that. She told me how smart I was and how pretty I was. She spent a lot of time praising me. That gave me more energy to work harder in school, to complete school, because now I know this little kid who is brilliant is in kindergarten. I didn't want to be going to college along with her.

I finally graduated from college. Sagashus was 8-years-old. That was my beginning of "now what do I do with myself?" I decided I was going to be a mother. That gave me time to spend with Sagashus, and that was another thing that got my son sad. I didn't give up anything for him, but I gave up all this for Sagashus. Not because I cared more for Sagashus at that time, but because I had changed as an individual.

There were a lot of mothers in our community who were great women. They needed help. They worked hard, but were single moms. Some were functional addicts. They took care of their children, kept clean homes, but they used drugs. Others were married, had husbands who loved and took care of their children, but these men were still whorish. As women, we had to stick together. So I took their children to the library to help them with reading. I helped those that wanted their GED get their GED. I helped others get their high school diploma, and some went on to college, and some went on and got their master's and PhDs. Some of the children really didn't

helped my daughter have a good life."

Another parent came to me. "Ms. Larry, why you educating my daughter? Now she won't come and see me." I explained to her that once they become educated, they are gonna leave the ghetto. They're gonna better their life. Any time children can take care of themselves, that means that you don't have to worry about taking care of them. They become independent. As time went on, these parents were happy I helped their children.

I became a founder of an organization called Genesis Housing Development Corporation to help low-income single parents find affordable homes. That was another way I gave back to the community. Also, I was allocated $150,000 from a foundation that told me do whatever

I believe in God, but I also believe that a person should never let someone else validate her. If you give that person the power to validate you, you also give **that person the power to control your happiness.**

have mothers that was giving them love and attention. I remembered when I was like that. My mother helped me with Bobby. She helped with Sagashus, and I had a supportive dad. But these ladies had no support. They just had these kids.

One parent asked me, "Why are you educating my daughter? I get disability for her. You educate her, I will lose out on my money." That particular child, she was 12-years-old, but she had a first grade academic level. I worked with her, and I worked with her, and I worked with her. She ended up graduating. As an adult, she has a good job, and she did a year or so of college. Now years have passed and her mom came back and said, "Ms. Larry, I really appreciate that you didn't listen to me. You

I wanted with it. I took that, and I got these boys who dropped out and I got them into construction training. For many, that was the first time they got paid for doing a job.

I am who I am today because I was able to ask God, and my son, to forgive me for being an abusive mother. In return, I was able to forgive myself, and that made me a better person, a better mother, a better grandmother, better aunt. It made me able to help children in the community.

I became a community mother to these children. They could always come to me and ask me for food when their mothers didn't have food, or they could come and ask me, when they were in jail, to pray for them. I would take them to ballets, expose them to some cultural experiences they normally wouldn't have in their lives.

One of my kids whose mom was a prostitute, he became a good father, and he says that was because of my help. I should have helped my own son more. Maybe he wouldn't have gone to jail. I helped a lot of other children in the community to keep them from going to jail. I showed them a better life, and I gave them the love they didn't get at home.

The bottom line is this: children, whether from their teacher, from their neighbor, or from a stranger, children thrive off love.

After how I treated my son, he never disrespected me. He never showed dislike or was angry with me for how I treated him. Now he has children, and he told his children they always have somebody that they can go and talk to. "Your grandma is always a good person to talk to when you're going through problems." Even though I treated him like I treated him, he still gave me respect. And he turned out to be an excellent dad. I can thank his dad for that. He was always there for him. Together, my son and I raised his children. They lived with us, in our home. And we, together, raised them as a team.

My superpower developed on this journey. It is never giving up. Always, always hold on to your dreams. Also, be responsible. Let me put it this way: be responsible for your faults, and own up to them. Do not take out your frustrations and your anger on other people and blame them for why you're not where you want to be.

You can't grow if you don't know where you messed up.

I believe in God, but I also believe that a person should never let someone else validate her. If you give that person the power to validate you, you also give that person the power to control your happiness.

Go inside yourself and see what you're doing wrong, and then correct yourself so you can grow. I'm able to look at myself and take responsibility for what I've done and not blame others for the person that I was. It was me that was being selfish, and I just thank the Lord and myself that I'm no longer a selfish person. ✤

Rakina

I didn't know my father was an alcoholic. I knew he would go to the tavern with his friend, Mr. Williams, and his other buddies, and they would have a "taste," as he called it. He worked nights. He was a chef and worked for an airline.

My sister, Oroki, and I grew up in the same house. She was four years older. He was mean to her and nicer to me. I never knew why. As a kid, it's like, cool! You know, this is great! Any time we would get in an argument, he would always favor me.

My parents divorced, and my mother remarried. She married another alcoholic. This man was physically abusive to her. I felt uncomfortable around him because I was 14, and when he first started coming to visit, he would have me sit on his lap. I didn't like it. Mostly what I hated, hated, hated was that he would get drunk and abuse my mother physically. I had to witness that, and I felt hopeless and helpless.

I stayed away a lot from home and ended up pregnant at 17. It was a difficult time. I stopped going to school. I'm a high school dropout and teen mother. My son was born in 1975. I'd just turned 18. Prior to that, what saved me and continued to give me hope was my involvement in the Chicago Black Arts and the Pan-African movements.

I went to the Chicago Public High School for Metropolitan Studies, also called Metro High School. It was known as the school without walls, kind of experimental. You had to apply and be accepted to get into Metro, and my sister encouraged me to try. We would come to one central place and get our bus tokens, and we had classes all over the city. I remember having a class in Playboy Towers, a writing class. You had to submit a writing sample to get into the class. Everybody wanted in because everybody wanted to go to Playboy Towers. I actually taught a class. Who would have thought that later I would drop out of high school? I was discovering my African identity, so I taught a class in black history. I remember feeling bad about having to give grades and not give everybody As.

After my parents divorced, we had a fire in our West Side apartment, and we moved in with my grandmother on the South Side. I was 11. We moved a lot after that. We were pretty unstable. We didn't have a lot of money. We were struggling. My mother was a single mother. In the community, there were people that I connected with, older people and people my age. When I was in high school, I joined an organization called the Black Body. We read books about black history, African history, and we had discussions. We met at a library on 35th and King Drive. We would do events, three or four a year around historical moments. We would have poetry, drama, African dance, and speeches to educate others about these occurrences. We had one for Marcus Garvey Day in August. We had one for Malcolm X. We studied a country in West Africa called Guinea. The people in Guinea fought against a Portuguese invasion, and they were able to maintain their independence. So we had the Guinea Invasion event.

Oroki and I became vegetarians. When my mother would make the greens for us, she didn't put the pork in there no more. She was supportive when we took African names. When she would come to the African events, she would wear an African dress like us.

Some people I knew started planning a trip to Ghana, and I wanted to go. That was in 1973, and I was 15. I sold jewelry in art fairs to make enough money to buy a plane ticket to go to Africa. I remembered being much younger and taking a trip to O'Hare Airport. At that time, they would let you sit on the plane and see what it felt like. I never ever thought that I would be able to fly, actually fly on a plane. But I saved money, and I was able to go on that trip to Africa. It was my first time flying on a plane.

It was such a shaky situation—me going to Ghana—because there was this man. He wasn't a boyfriend. We weren't sexually active. He said that you can stay with my family when you go to Ghana. The trip was a charter just for airfares, so people had to make their own living arrangements when they got there. His family was not in the capital, Accra, but in Kumasi, about four hours away. Somehow the charter date was changed by a day, and I left a day late. I don't remember where he was, but I wasn't able to tell him, and he wasn't able to tell his family, so nobody was there to pick me up from the airport. An older friend of mine, Akosua, said, "Take this number. This is the family I met when I went to Ghana." She had gone a few years before. "You could probably stay with them for a night or two." They were in Accra.

I remember being at this phone booth in the airport and calling this family with my friend Aki, who's 18. She and I were going to be together wherever we were going to end up. We were supposed to go to Kumasi together.

They answered, and we said, "Well, we're stranded, and can we come and stay with you all?" We stayed with them the whole time, pretty much. Both of us later went to Kumasi for a few days. The family in Accra was very, very kind to us. They were somewhat well-off. The father was a retired barrister. That's like a judge. And he had his daughter, Lily, who was 18, the same age as Aki. Lily revealed to us that her father had seven wives. And this was a Christian family. Two wives lived in the house, and the other five were somewhere in the neighborhood. We went to visit one of them, and she was a Queen Mother. I wasn't sure why they called her Queen Mother, but it sounded important. Their ethnic group was Ewe. Platform shoes were in style then, and afros. But the Queen Mother had to dress in traditional dress, "no platforms," which the people in Ghana called "guaranteed shoes," and no European dresses.

Finally, I connected with my friend Akwasi's family in Kumasi, and I wanted to go there and meet them. And so we went to the bus station. I carried this big bag on my shoulder everywhere I went. It had a map of Africa, neon colors, bright, and the bag was black. On top of the bag was my wallet. Just right on top. This man was pushing up against me and… Anyway, my wallet was stolen. I had nothing. I didn't have much in the beginning, but now I had nothing. That family that didn't even know me, that graciously opened their home—now I had to borrow money from them! When I got back to Chicago, I mailed them the money.

The house in Kumasi was more traditional, like a compound, a big yard with houses all around. Aki got sick. She was vomiting and vomiting and vomiting. I got sick there, too. I remember going to the toilet a lot, and the toilets were shared by others in the compound. They were pretty disgusting.

Aki and I were in the Black Body Dancers back in Chicago. In Accra, we were hanging out with people from the university. They took us to this nightclub called the Napoleon Club. Their house band became quite famous because they did an album with Hugh Masekela, a famous South African trumpet player. They were having a record release party, and they said, "Well, yeah, we're having this big party, and you all can dance, and we'll pay you." We did our little dance on a big stage. People said we were on TV after that. They paid us, not much—like 10 cedis, which is very little money—but we were living off whatever we had, so it helped.

I have to tell about my good friend Jahnali. He was older than me. He was in college, I was in high school. We never had an intimate relationship or anything like that. He made his own flutes, and he made this instrument called panpipes, both from bamboo. Jahnali played with Phil Cohran and the Black Music Ensemble. At 15, I was going to jazz shows and sets—we called them sets. Jahnali and I became good friends. He once told me he was going to be my best friend. We hung out together and often shared a table at art fairs, he selling his flutes and panpipes, and me selling earrings. He taught me how to play panpipes. Jahnali went to Ghana also, with his friend BoBo, who is Oscar Brown III. Bobo was one of Chicago's greatest bass players, who died tragically in a car crash in 1996. On the way back from Ghana, Jahnali was sick on the plane. Eventually, he got malaria and died. I was crushed. He was like the first person who was close to me who died. I remember being in the parking lot after his funeral, and I couldn't stop crying. The only reason why Aki and I ended up having some malaria tablets is that we rode to New York with this older couple who were also going on the trip, and they talked to us about malaria. They had some extra pills, and they gave us these pills,

and we took them. We got lucky. But my best friend, Jahnali, got malaria, and he died.

When I came back from Ghana, it was the same situation, or worse, at home. The abuse was worse. I met my son's father, who was from Ghana. I hung out at his house. It was just somewhere to go. I don't think that I was in love with him. I had sex, and I got pregnant.

I stopped going to school. But I felt like I should be responsible, so I started reading about being a parent. I breastfed my son. The three of us lived together, and tried to be a family. We had an apartment, and he didn't have a lot of money. My grandmother got him a job working at the pillow factory. My mother worked there, too. I didn't know him well, and he didn't really know me well. But we tried. It didn't work out. We lived together for three years, and I realized at some point, I don't even know this person, and that he was not the person I wanted to be with.

I got back in school and passed the GED. My aunt, who was a nurse's aide, got me my first job, as a nurse's aide at South Shore Hospital. I did it because I needed to support my son. If I had thought about it, maybe I would have done something in college like English or creative writing. To this day, that's my true love. My son's father got me listening to reggae music, and I remember playing Rastaman Vibration by Bob Marley over and over on the record player in our raggedy one-bedroom apartment on the South Side. Between that and Stevie Wonder's Songs in the Key of Life, I wore out that little record player. I started liking reggae music a lot and later, after my son's father and I split up, I would go out to nightclubs.

When my son was little, my sister and some other families formed an independent black school. We decided we wanted to educate our own children but not homeschool. The school was in a storefront. My son's

father got involved, probably because I kind of forced him to, and all the other parents did, too. We tried to teach our children to know and love themselves and their African heritage. My son did pre-school and kindergarten there. Unfortunately, the school eventually had to close.

I don't remember what age my son became a latchkey kid. A lot of times I was working evenings, so he would come home and I was already gone to work. He was alone a lot. I didn't leave him home alone when he was really, really young; I had babysitters. But I wasn't available for him a lot because I was either working or going out to the reggae clubs. I started going on trips to Jamaica, and I took him with me. I met this family in Jamaica, Mr. Percy and Miss Sylvie. And they had grandchildren that were my son's age. I would leave my son with them and then go party.

My son attended many different schools. He attended another independent black school in Chicago and later transferred to a private school where my sister was teaching. We moved from the South Side to the North Side of the city, and he attended public school for the first time. By then, he wasn't doing well in school. I know it was because I wasn't there for him, giving him the time he needed, helping him with homework and all that stuff. When he was in fifth grade, he was struggling, and so I decided to transfer him to a Catholic school, thinking that might help. I didn't really pay much attention to him when he was in high school. I was working and partying. After he graduated from high school, I got him into a program that supported him to attend college at Northeastern University. By that time, I was about to move from Chicago to Wisconsin, but I hadn't done what I needed to do as a parent to help my son be independent and successful in college. It would be much later before my eldest son would graduate from college.

I met my second husband, who's my ex-husband now, while traveling in Trinidad. He was born in the Caribbean. I was still living in Chicago. I went to visit, and a friend of a friend introduced us. We were both visiting, and we were attracted to each other and shared similar views. He went back home to the UK and I back to Chicago, but we communicated via long letters and phone calls. Back then, there was no Viber or WhatsApp, so those phone calls were expensive. And I spent hours on the phone, further neglecting my son, who really needed me during those times.

I fell hard in love with him. There were red flags for me, and we debated on many topics via those letters and calls. I felt our love was stronger than any disagreements we had, and I believed I could change him... yeah, right. Love is blind! During our marriage, we separated and got back together so many times. We stayed together about eight years altogether, and I had another son with him. During our separations, I would see other people, and he did, too. One time, after we had gotten back together for the umpteenth time, he told me had a 4-year-old child in another town. It hurt me to think that I had been left out of that for so many years.

Today, we're still friends. He's still in Chicago, and my son is very close to him. I had my second son at 31. My kids are 13 years apart. With my second son, I made different choices. I was older, and it was a planned pregnancy. I was involved in his academics and his school— volunteering at the school and going to all the meetings. I had gotten my LPN license while I was with my first husband, and later, I realized oh, but there's such a thing as a registered nurse. So I got my associate's degree at a community college, and while I was with my second husband, I decided I needed a bachelor's degree. So I did a BSN, bachelor of science in nursing. This might sound like it was easy, but it was hard, working, going to school and partying... because I had to party. Music was like air to me. I needed it, and I tried my best to involve my kids, taking them with me when I could, but they didn't allow kids in the reggae clubs. I slowed down on the partying a little bit after my second son was born, but I once snuck him into a reggae concert at the Park West, a club on the North Side of Chicago. He was hidden in his baby carrier buttoned up under my trench coat! Think that's why both of my kids love music so much to this day.

My first labor and delivery nurse job was at Northwestern. I didn't like Northwestern because I thought they discriminated against poor people. They had what they called the service patients—the ones that had public aid. I thought they didn't treat patients equally, so I didn't work there very long.

I wanted to work in Provident Hospital on the South Side because it was a black-owned hospital. It was established by an African American physician, Dr. Daniel Hale Williams, and was the first African American-owned and operated hospital in the United States. I was proud to get a job there as a registered nurse in labor and delivery.

In 1987, some people I know told me about this trip to Libya. I had continued to work in organizations. After Black Body, I joined another Pan-African organization. So I was actively studying and working within an organization, and had lots of connections to other activists. The Libya trip was in 1987, before I got pregnant with my second son. I was working at Provident, and it was a year after the United States bombed Libya. There were about 200 people from the US who went, black and white, and there were about 100 from Canada and 100 from the UK. It was totally paid for by the government of Libya.

To get out of work, I created a death. I really wanted to go. Libya was beautiful. When I think about what's happening in Libya now, I'm so sad. We were at the hotel, and they woke us up in the middle of the night and took us to Gaddafi's house. The timing coincided with exactly the same time the US dropped the bombs, only one year later. When the US bombed Libya in 1986, it was Gaddafi's house that was bombed. The US missiles were sitting in the yard. Gaddafi and his wife had adopted a little girl. She was 16 months old, and she was killed in the bombing. They took us to her room, and there was her little picture on the wall, along with toys scattered about. Everybody came out of that house crying.

When we came back, by way of Rome, they took away our passports. You weren't supposed to go to Libya; there was a travel ban. We were taken into a room and the authorities were speaking Italian; it was pretty scary. Eventually they let us go. When we got back out into the airport, the main area, they said that there was no flight back. I was getting more anxious. I hung out with the people from the UK. The group I hung out with were people from the Caribbean, immigrants to London. There was this one who was a musician, and he sang a song about the Jamahiriya—that's what they called the revolution in Libya when Gaddafi came to power. So in Rome, I went to the airline and I said, "Can I just go to the UK?" You know, because they were leaving. They weren't going to be delayed.

I didn't need a visa to go to London. I stayed for two days in London, and then I came back to New York. I didn't have any problems like the others from the US who were detained and questioned extensively about the trip to Libya.

An African American woman was the dean of the school of nursing where I got my bachelor's degree. I was finishing up that degree when I got pregnant with my second son. That was the summer of '88. It was tough, and I was struggling with my pregnancy and clinical rotations. The dean at some point was like, "Maybe you should take the semester off." But I was determined to graduate with my class, and I just persevered. I graduated on time with my class, proudly carrying my son on my hip as I walked across the stage.

My mother always supported me through my marriage, divorce, and drama with men. And she believed in serving others in spite of everything that she was going through. My mother always helped other people. She finally, finally got the strength to leave my stepfather. He

ally got the hang of breastfeeding and breastfed my son for 16 months. Later, as an RN, I worked mostly in labor and delivery. I saw many young, teen moms in hospitals in Chicago who were just like me, and I connected with them and tried to advocate for them.

Currently I work in college health. I'm a women's health nurse practitioner. At the student health clinic on campus, I do pelvic exams, Pap tests and STI screening, and I have prescriptive authority. I also educate young women about their bodies and try to assist my patients with empowering themselves to be advocates for themselves and their health.

No one really encouraged me verbally, but the images and other women who were around me helped me to know that I could make something out of my life.

took the house, and she didn't fight him. At some point, she stopped working at the pillow factory. She had heart disease. She struggled financially and emotionally.

My mother also spoke fluent Spanish. She learned Spanish on her job because she worked with a lot of Mexican people. She loved everyone, and she would always be doing nice things for her Mexican friends. They all just loved her. Everyone loved my mother.

Doing for others came from my mother. But the decision to go into women's health was a conscious decision because, as a teen mom, I went through hardship with my son, including the stigma of being a teen mother and not getting respect or support from healthcare workers who I believe felt I'd never amount to anything. When I decided to breastfeed, I had a hard time initially, and the nurses' solution was to bring in formula. But I eventu-

I want to work more with other women of African descent because I feel like there's a great need in our community. I want to share with other sisters the knowledge and the skills and the passion that I have for African American women's health. In 2012, I applied to the Global Health Institute to do a Capstone in global health. Part of the requirements was to do a field experience at the end of the program. I really wanted to go to Burkina Faso because I had visited there. But in The Gambia they speak English, and in Burkina Faso they speak French, so I decided to do my field experience in The Gambia.

I'm 59 now, and I reflect back to that time in my life that was the most difficult for me—when I was pregnant as a teenager and I dropped out of school. I thought of ending my life back then, but I'm so glad I didn't. I believe the Creator has a purpose for me in life, and I'm now trying to live my passion and my dreams. I think about other girls who are in similar situations now, and I feel a need to share my story because perhaps it will help someone gain the strength and courage to go on. I saw this young sister on the bus the other day with a little baby, and she was very young. She was a teenager. The baby was crying loud, and people were moving. I sat next to her, and I started playing with the baby, and the baby calmed down. I was thinking about what her life was like. My mother died of a heart attack at 67. I used to think 67 was old, but now that I'm almost 60, 67 is not old. I have a lot to do, and I believe I'll have many more years to do stuff, God willing.

Between 2014 and 2015, I traveled to West Africa and volunteered with Starfish International, an organization in The Gambia that provides access to education for girls. Starfish isn't a school, but they provide academic support after school and on weekends and they have a summer program. I taught sexual reproductive health to a group of 20 girls who are peer health educators. That means they educate other girls, and entire communities, on health and wellness. I believe that adolescent girls are so powerful, and those girls in The Gambia are making a difference in the lives of others. I went back in 2015 and continue to work with them. I was invited to be on the board of an organization called the Inter-African Committee. This organization fights against traditional practices that threaten women's health, such as female genital mutilation (FGM). I have friends who have gone through FGM, and the long-term physical and emotional consequences are devastating. Getting involved with IAC will mean taking some trips to DC to work with them. I'm very excited about this.

In Guinea, 97 to 98 percent of women have undergone female genital mutilation. Can you imagine? I thought about that statistic… I know people from Guinea. I never really talked to them about it. In The Gambia they just recently banned it. People still do it under the table. It happens in the US, too. There are people here that are doing it, so it's not just happening in Africa and the Middle East. And there are many women globally who are suffering from the psychological and physical consequences of FGM.

Music is still very, very important to me. It helps me in what I'm feeling. I need to be uplifted. And faith is very important to me. I meditate. Now that I'm fasting, I'm meditating and praying more. Although I'm not Muslim, I decided to fast during Ramadan in 1998-99. The day I broke that first fast, January 19, 1999, I got back to work after having lunch with a friend, and I got a call. My mom had passed away. I was able to handle that news, even though it was devastating, because I felt stronger spiritually because I had just come off that fast. In honor of my mother, and for my physical and spiritual health, I fast every year for Ramadan. I also do it in honor of my many Muslim friends and Muslims everywhere, including my best friend Amie Joof, who was from The Gambia and passed away in 2010.

My superpower is telling my story. Telling my story might be through writing. It might be through speaking. It might be through working with other girls and women where I tell my story in order to have an impact on their lives. People ask me what inspired me to be a nurse, and I talk about my Aunt Esther, and I talk about the TV show Julia. Some of you may remember that show. She was the first black woman professional I remember seeing on TV. Diahann Carroll played the role. She wore the nurse hat. She worked. She was a single mother. No one really encouraged me verbally, but the images and other women who were around me helped me to know that I could make something out of my life. I became self-motivated. I'm sure my mother was proud of me when she came to my graduations. I got a writing award at one graduation, and I was acknowledged. I invited my mother, and she came, along with my sister and my grandmother.

When I went to The Gambia to work with the girls the second year, and I said, "We haven't been together for a year. Tell me what's going on in your lives." About half of the girls had a story about a baby that died—their sister's baby, their aunt's baby, or someone's. Infant mortality is very, very high in many places in Africa, including The Gambia. One girl told the story of her aunt trying to have a kid. She would get pregnant; she would lose the baby many, many times. The last time she lost the baby, she died also. The second year I taught the girls how to make oral rehydration solution. Oral rehydration solution is a way of providing the right balance of electrolytes for a child that has diarrhea and is dehydrated. It's just fluid and electrolytes they need to survive. It's simple, and they're now able to make it. They have also shown the women in their village who come to the Bantaba— a community gathering—how to make it. Last year, the class was about breastfeeding exclusively for the first six months. That's so important in The Gambia and in countries where there's no access to clean water. Women tend to give babies water

because it's hot, and they think babies need water. They don't understand that breast milk can provide all the fluids and nutrients the baby needs. We visited the National Nutrition Agency—NaNA. We discovered that the curriculum they were using was the same as what we were doing in class. That was affirming for me and the girls. The girls are continuing to learn and teach others, and I am so proud of them. They all speak at least two languages— English and whatever their native language is—and many of them speak three. They deliver their education in whatever language the women (or men, as they educate the entire village) speak. They're making a huge difference in the lives of women. And girls.

I am about to embark on a new journey in my life. I'll be living and working in Africa for one year starting in July 2017. Maybe I'll extend it. I'll be a nurse educator, working with students through an organization that is striving to increase the health capacity of healthcare workers on the continent. Ever since I was 15 and took that first trip to Africa, I have wanted to go back and serve the people in some meaningful way. My sons are grown up and living their lives; I am proud to say that they both have college degrees and are productive members of society. Africa is the land of my ancestors. I feel a responsibility. And I am so excited. ✤

Twjuana

My mother did not always have an addiction. She had a nervous breakdown during my teens, and that's the point at which she lost it. She struggled for many years, but she's okay now.

Before her breakdown, my life wasn't all roses. My father was verbally, emotionally, and mentally abusive. I didn't have any peace. Some people could deal with that, but I internalized all the messages that came with it. I was very unhappy. Growing up in a family of Bible thumpers and drug addicts didn't make it any better. I didn't have anyone to turn to. There were no intellectuals. The only one we had, he was an alcoholic. But at least I had my mom. When she started to self-destruct, I was like, shit, that sealed the deal for me. Those things were supposed to make me a horrible mother, but they actually made me stronger.

When I was homeless and sleeping on my auntie's couch, my three younger cousins were there. I often remind them they brought me back to life, because I would play games and watch TV with them when they were kids, and their innocence revived me. That started my journey to reconnect with my family.

In 2003, 2004 I started a tradition of an annual Christmas party. We've been doing it every year since. I've watched how my family has become closer and how the party has gotten bigger and how it sets an example for everyone. It has impacted my family, I believe.

I would like to have a greater impact on the community at large with a not-for-profit. I'm currently working on purchasing a property for that.

Being a strong mom for me means providing a safe space for my daughter to be able to be who she is. It's important for me to not alter her natural self. When I say that, I mean it's important if she's going to be loud and bossy for me to allow her to be a loud and bossy girl, but also teach her what comes with that. I don't want to change who she is. If she wants to wear cowgirl boots and a tutu to school, I want her to be able to do that.

Being a strong mom for me means being able to let my baby be who she is, but in addition to that, creating a safe space for her to communicate to me about anything she's thinking about so that she will always feel supported. I'm teaching her to count on me as her sounding board.

I had to create my own home. It took me 36, 37, however many years I've been on this earth, to create a home. I never had one when I was younger.

When I left for boarding school and I went home on the weekends, I went to the place where my family lived, but it didn't feel like a home. We moved around a lot when I was younger because my parents were poor. They worked hard but never bought a house. After they separated, we moved around even more. Then after I left and went to college and came back to Chicago, I moved around a lot because I was poor.

I finally bought a house, and I feel stable now. I have a knack for creating things and building things, so I was able to get this structure and then build myself into it. That's why I took the picture with the drill, because it represents me finally having a place I can call home that I can always go to, a place in which my daughter has lived her entire life. This is the only home that she knows. She's comfortable here. It's hers, and she thinks it's beautiful. I never felt like that when I was her age.

My sister lives upstairs and my niece lives upstairs. It's a family building. It's rough sometimes, but it's nice to know that my niece is in a safe place, a clean place, that my sister can afford.

I am who I am today because I've gone through the belly of the beast.

The belly of the beast for me represents... I don't know—how old am I? I'll be 39. I've owned this place for three years. So about 35, 36 years of feeling like I was in a rubber room. I joke and I say that I'm going to get an extra 30 years at the end of my life because the first 30 were so fucked up.

finished my bachelor's degree, which made it easier for me to buy my building. I went back to my old job, which helped me get my current job. I'm now outside of the beast's belly.

I would not change any of it. Maybe I would change some of it, but most of it I would keep just the way it is, because I think fighting every day made me build up a whole lot of muscle which I can now impart to my daughter. She's a little version of me; it's almost like I was her martyr.

The struggle is always alive. It never dies. I'm going to forever carry those things with me, those big demons, the things that make me uncomfortable, the things that still cause me to have social anxiety sometimes or to fear being in groups of people I don't know, or being self-conscious, overthinking, or feeling like I have a foggy head and I can't speak. Those things are always going to be

I felt caged for so long. Now I feel free. I don't feel caged anymore.

My self-hatred began very early on. It feels like the devil tried to kill me right away and pulled out all the stops to try to make it happen. The ongoing battle between the outside forces and my instincts and my desires and my wants to have a certain kind of a life—that struggle made life really, really difficult for me.

All I ever wanted was to do well, to get good grades in school, get a good job, and be a regular person. But it was always the hardest thing in the world for me to do those things. I never could do well in school because I had so much emotional baggage.

Going through the belly of the beast is like fighting every day, all day for 35 years, and not giving up. With a lot of prayer and asking for guidance, I started to unfold; the fruits of my labor, they started to bloom. I finally

alive. What has died is the notion that I was forsaken. I felt forsaken for so long. I could not understand why my shit was so fucked up. I don't feel forsaken anymore.

What came to life is my creative spirit. It's more alive than it's ever been. I'm finally able to do all the things I wanted to do as a child. I always felt like a painter without a paintbrush, or a prodigy musician with no instrument and not even a box to bang on. I always had this urge.

You know, when I was little, I used to change my room around all the time. I loved colors, and I would make collages. I would go to the auto show and take all the magazines and stick them all over my walls all different kinds of way. Nobody ever said, "Hey, maybe you might like interior design." I didn't know there was a thing for it. I wanted to take dance classes, and I wanted to be a singer, and I wanted to be a performer, and I wanted to be on stage and be expressive. But my parents never put me in the dance classes.

I felt caged for so long. Now I feel free. I don't feel caged anymore. And that's what's completely alive. I feel like the world is my oyster. It only took 40 years for me to be able to manifest all that I want.

Callie Décor is a home décor boutique I've been dreaming about for more than 10 years. I named it after my maternal grandmother and my great-grandmother; they're both named Callie, however, they're not related. My grandfather's mother's name was Callie and he married a Callie. I figured there had to be something special about that name and that I would pay homage to my grandmother and my great-grandmother, especially since I look exactly like my great-grandmother.

I'm planning to open Callie Décor in the spring of 2018. I'm also going to have Callie Décor Social, which will be the non-profit side of Callie Décor, whereby children can come and engage in visual arts and dance and theater and things of that nature.

My experiences with feeling stuck in a box and not able to express myself pushes me to provide that outlet for others, which is why I let my baby... You know, she has paintbrushes and paint because she loves to do that stuff. She loves to dance. So yeah, I want other kids to be able to do that, too.

I've learned how to be invisible. I don't know when

I learned how to do it. It has gotten me out of trouble, but it has also shown me that I'm covered by God's grace and mercy. Being invisible has made stuff happen that I don't think would typically happen. It has made miracles happen in my life.

But I think my superpower is resilience. Maybe that's my superpower: resilience. Sometimes when you've been knocked down, and you're hurting, and you feel hopeless, and you can't even get off the bed, it is a superpower just to keep going.

A superpower doesn't have to mean you can scale tall buildings, right? When your shit is fucked up, and you don't have any money, and you don't have any food, or whatever is going to bring you some anxiety at the end of the day because you can't do it, and it's based on heartache—getting out the bed requires superpower. Or figuring out how you're going to spread your money out takes superpower.

I think it's important that people understand that as infamous mothers we conquer, we improve, we teach, we learn. But by no means am I saying that I have corrected all my ills and that I'm a perfect being and that I don't struggle. When people think of motherhood, they think of perfect people, and we're not perfect. It's a constant struggle—or a constant pursuit—to become better, and I just wanted that to be noted. Maybe that's why we're infamous, because we're constantly striving.

In a world that's always pretending moms are perfect, what makes us infamous is—we don't pretend. Yeah. ✽

Lenora

I am a mother, grandmother, great-grandmother, a wife, and a woman of faith, and I feel that that's pretty infamous. I never thought that I would even live to see my daughter become a woman, but not only have I seen her become a grown woman, I have also had the pleasure of playing a part in my grandchildren's and great-grandchildren's lives.

When I was like a year or two years, someone gave me some type of medication, and I fell through the screen door, and I was injured. I carried the scar on my stomach mostly all my life from that injury. My auntie came and took me from Chicago because someone tried to kill me. I was dirty and hungry, and all I knew was hotdogs because that is what I was fed, along with sugar milk. I grew up in a very violent household in which my uncles were forever fighting and beating up on someone. I lived in fear. When I got old enough to make decisions for myself, they ended up being all bad decisions because I decided to start using drugs, amongst other things.

I never knew my father, and my mother was—and I'm not blaming her for anything because I made my own decisions—a dysfunctional alcoholic, and I got little or no attention. I spent a lot of time by myself. And I was looking for love and only found sex because I had no idea what love was because I wasn't shown love. I did the things that I needed to do to get the attention that I thought I needed. I didn't know any better. It led me from man to man, sexually transmitted diseases, drug abuse, living in abandoned buildings. You name it, I've been through it.

My grandmother took us to church all the time, and I knew that there was a God. No matter what happened, no matter what I went through, I always believed that there was a God, and I also believed that He only wanted the best for me. As a matter of fact, when I used to get high, I used to tell the people that I was getting high with, "Y'all better enjoy this because I'm not going to be here with you all much longer." And they would always ask me, "Where are you going?" I'd be like, "I don't know. But I know one thing. I'm not going to be getting high, and I'm not going to be here with y'all because this isn't what God wants for me." And I knew this truth deep down in my heart.

Finally, I was sick and tired of being sick and tired, so I went to my gynecologist because I didn't know anything about NA, AA or no other recovery program, and I told him I had a drug problem, and the bottom line is if I have to continue to get high, I want to die. I did not want to live. And he was looking at me like, "Lenora, I don't know anything about drug addiction. Just sit here." When I was sitting there he walked out the room and he locked the door, and I noticed I couldn't get out. And he was gone about an hour, hour and a half, and when he came back he said, "You know, I talked to my colleagues, and they told me that I should lock you up. I should have you committed because you said that you did not want to live... you'd rather die than to continue to get high. But you know what? There's something in you. I can't put my finger on it, but I cannot send you to a mental institution because you're not crazy, so I am going to send you to a recovery facility, and you cannot be released unless it is to a recovery home." And this is where my journey of recovery began.

He sent me to this exclusive place so I could detox. He told them, "Don't let her out. Don't worry about the money. And don't let her out of there until she has a recovery home to go to." The power of God at work.

I think about how far I've come.

You know, like I said, I never expected to even be here today with six grandchildren and six great-grandchildren. That's a blessing. I was not a good mother. I had my child at the age of 14, and I let my mother, who had neglected me, raise my daughter. Funny how the cycle of madness continues on and on unless it is plucked out by its roots. But I got a chance to help with the development of my grandchildren, and also I got to help my great-grandchildren.

I'm not the woman I used to be. I'm married, and the man that I am married to has his doctorate, and I have friends that have their doctorates. I'm in church regularly, and I just started a book club. I work regularly, and my life is just really good. And I'm happy.

I lived in Illinois, and I didn't have a high school diploma, but I owned a business—Granny's Cleaning Services—licensed—still licensed here in Madison.

My business was me and my family—my grandsons—and they're in Illinois. I was also a property manager, and worked with DCFS for over ten years with foster kids and watching kids of foster parents. I went on to take the test GED and passed, and now I have successfully completed two semesters of the 2014-2015 UW-Madison Odyssey Project. I earned college credits in the humanities.

We studied English, literature, art history, philosophy, American history, plus writing and critical thinking.

I'm writing a book. It's a book of poems.

My superpower is working with women and empowering women and letting them see who they are—because, for some reason, I can see who they are. Sometimes we don't know who we are, and we need someone to tell us who we can be. I like doing that because I never had that. And I know that it's something that's needed because I felt like maybe, just maybe, my life wouldn't have been as chaotic as it was when I was younger if I had someone to show me who I was—and also to guide and direct me. I'm not blaming anyone, because, like I said, when we get a certain age and we begin to make choices, we have to also be responsible for the choices we make. And there are consequences behind all of the choices that we make.

I started really early, at an early age, telling women: "Oh, you're beautiful. Oh, you look nice. Oh, I like your hair!" You know, just complimenting. That made me decide to write a poem "Why Not Tell You."

...funny how the cycle of madness continues on and on **unless it is plucked out by its roots.**

Why Not Tell You?

Why Not Tell You? That the truth you perceive to be true may not be accurate, or that maybe we need to take another look through new lenses or another pair of eyes. Are we, in reality, afraid of the truth? Is it because like Socrates says "that we are comfortable in our ignorance," or are we afraid that once we have been made aware of the truth that we will come out of the dark to never enter it again, only to be present in the light? Then what?

Why Not Tell You? That you are smarter way beyond your most vivid dreams or your wildest imaginations, or are you like one of the people in the "Allegory of the Cave" that were physically and mentally bound and refused to let another free them because they were convinced that their interpretation of what they saw was absolute?

Why Not Tell You? That you are beautiful and deserving of all that is good. Is it because you are so use to believing and living by the negative adjective used to describe your very existence?

Why Not Tell You? That you are great. Is it because you are afraid that you might end up on a predestined date with greatness, a date that you do not believe that you are worthy of or even deserve?

Why Not Tell You? That after this UW Odyssey there awaits a greater one that will last a lifetime. Should I not tell you this because you would quit this journey that you are on right now in hope that life's challenges will not find you?

Why Not Tell You? All of these wonderful things about yourself. Are you afraid that if you let go of whom you think you are that you might become the person that you were really meant to be?

Why Not Tell You?

(L. J.R)

Women are the only human beings that were not created out of dirt from the earth. Adam was created out of dirt from the earth. We were created out of flesh and bone. The man said, "This is now bone of my bones, And flesh of my flesh; She shall be called Woman Because she was taken out of Man." We bring forth life. A Woman gave birth to the Messiah. A Woman gave birth to the King and Queens of the world, and a Woman gave birth to our presidents—now tell me that isn't infamous.

When I was asked what I thought about Infamous Mothers, the picture of the Tomb of the Unknown Soldier came to mind. Mothers' and women's forgotten dreams and tears unseen. Mothers' and women's unheard voices, silenced by their struggle to survive their screams, are but a whimper in the wind, and their scars are forever hidden and masked by the need to put food on the table.

Infamous Mothers has given us a face, a voice. We get to be heard. We can be seen. It is possible to survive motherhood and life. I thank God for Infamous Mothers because without this platform, our lives would have never been told, and our voices would have never been heard, and our tears would have been in vain.

Thank you, S. Levingston, for your dream, because without it, ours would have perished.

Mrs. Lenora Rodin ✲

Edwina

I start with Chicago. I was a chronic runaway. I did not like being with my family. They wouldn't let me do whatever I wanted to do, and I always wanted to do my thing.

I was selling drugs to have a place to stay. I went to this lady house name Ms. Marie, and she let me stay there because I was dating her son. I was 15, and he was 19. She said, "Baby you need to go with your people because you can't stay here in my house. And I know you're sleeping with my son. And I don't want to get in trouble because you are a minor." Ms. Marie got in touch with my grandfather, and he said, "Send her to me." He got the ticket, and they put me on a Greyhound bus.

My grandfather expected a 15-year-old girl. When I got off the bus, my grandfather was standing there looking. He say, "What happened to you?" "Nothing, this is me." He said, "I thought you was a grown woman." I said, "No, sir." He took me home and said, "You know you got to get to school." He had no idea that I was a runaway. I was smoking weed. I was having sex. I was doing acid. He's looking for a little girl, his granddaughter.

My sister was already in New Orleans. She was grown, and her name was also Marie. One day we were going to pay bills. We stopped at this place called Ellie, where you could eat po'boy sandwiches and drink and dance. We met this guy she was dating. He had his friend with him, and they introduced me to him. He had no idea I was 15. I got full of alcohol. We went to the hotel. Well, you know what happened.

My grandfather was steaming hot mad at me and my sister. He said it didn't take that long to pay no damn bills. About six weeks passed, I was throwing up. I found out I was pregnant. My grandfather said, "We'll, you're having this baby. Your teenage years are over." I had the baby. My neighbor took me to the hospital. At the time, the buses and the cabs were on strike. That was in 1975, September. I'll never forget that.

When I came back home from the hospital, I was told, "Your sister ain't going to help you take care of that baby. I don't babysit. That baby is with you 24/7." I had to get up at five o'clock in the a.m. to have the diapers out by six, and I had to boil the bottles. Back then they had Pampers, but I didn't have none.

I did that for so long, then my grandfather started getting up with the baby in the morning. My grandfather's name was Samuel. So I named my son Samuel. Once Sam started crawling, my grandfather would pick him up in the mornings and let me sleep. When I'd wake up in the morning, they'd be eating toast. You know how old people dip their bread in the coffee? That's what they'd be doing. And Sam's feet would just be going.

One day, I went to take out the trash and met my son's father. I got pregnant with my second boy. My grandfather said, "Don't you take out no more damn garbage because you come back pregnant."

My second son's father used to fight me. He would hit me, and I just fly across the room. He beat me so bad

I was taking an ass whooping like a grown woman. Then he apologize, saying he wasn't going to do it anymore. All this came from his mother not seeing me at the OB/GYN, and I got a whipping for that. Then I told him I was pregnant. That next morning when he got up to go to work, my neighbor next door said, "Girl, I heard you screaming last night. Let me call your family." I couldn't see, both eyes closed. My nose was broken. My lips were big. I got to my grandfather's house. My grandfather looked at me and said, "I'm going to kill 'im. I'ma kill 'im." I stay there with my grandfather. I did without prenatal care until my seventh month.

I made my mind up to go to the clinic. I don't know who told my son's father or how he found out, but he met me at the clinic. He said, "Bitch, come on before I knock your ass out of here." He took me to his house, and I told him the doctor said I couldn't have any sex due to my trauma with my baby since I never had prenatal care. He had sex with me anyway, and it was not enjoyable. I went home. I started bleeding, and they rushed me to the hospital. Sure enough, after the placenta came out first, they had to do an emergency C-section.

Calvin was born December 1, 1976. He was three pounds and 9-1/2 ounces. They said he wasn't going to make it after three days if he could not breathe on his own. April 1977, my grandfather passed away. So I had no more protection. My sister was scared of my son's father. After the funeral, I had to go live with Calvin. I couldn't get an apartment on my own. I was only 17-years-old and still considered a runaway.

Living with Calvin's father, I wasn't allowed to go to the door when he was home, or when he was not home. If the glasses weren't sitting a certain way, I got a beating. The kids crying, making too much noise, I had to shut them up, or I got a beating. He put me at the foot of the bed like a little dog while he slept. That was my life. I was 17.

I don't know the men his dad was hanging with. They broke into this lady's house next door to me. The lady had one little boy, must've been about 7. Well, they beat her and raped her in front of her son. The little boy identified my son's father and some other man. When the police came, they arrested him. He went down for 14 years. That's how God delivered me.

But before that I got into some trouble. My son's father got into it with someone across the apartment complex. He had a double-barrel shotgun. He got the shotgun and went over there and fired in the man's front door. My neighbor had a little small baby and when the shot came through, the mom had just taken the baby out of the bassinet, thank God, or that baby would have been dead.

My son's father ran and placed the gun underneath the sofa. The guy called the police, and they came and knocked on the door. I said, "I don't know nothin' about no gun." He said, "Ma'am, you know when we find that gun in here, you're going to jail." I said, "Yes, sir."

Even though I was 17, the lease and the light bill was in my name. I don't remember how that happened. The police found the gun. They charged me with accessory after the fact of attempted murder because I didn't tell them that I knew about the gun. My sister got my kids. I went to jail for two weeks until they found out that I had nothing to do with it. The guy my son's father shot at, he came and got me out of jail. He became my boyfriend.

That didn't last long because I didn't like the sex. After that, my baby daddy went to jail for 14 years. When I saw him again, I was living with a woman. I hadn't had my daughter yet.

I went to the Job Corps in Texas, and that was in '79. I got pregnant in 1980. While I was in Job Corps, I met this girl named Lady Z. She was gay. She told me, "You're going to be mine one day." I'm like, "No, I'm not." But she gave me comfort, and it went on from there.

In the process of that, I had to rush back to New Orleans because there was a fire in my kids' father's mother's house. My kids' father's mother was burnt up with another one of her grandchildren. I ended up coming home.

I was still running back and forth to Texas because Lady Z stayed in Houston. My sister, she drank a little bit, but I left my kids with her, and she lived with this lady, Ms. Millie. I left my boys to be with Lady Z.

After the fire, I graduated from Job Corps and came home with a nurse's aide certificate. I was supposed to get my GED, but I never did. After that I went to Texas, and I applied to go to the Army. I had to have my birth certificate, and I had to have someone write a letter stating they take care of my children while I was gone.

I went to Chicago to get my birth certificate but I ended up going out. I was high, real drunk. I remember waking up the next day and my pants were down. I go back to Texas to do my physical for the Army, and I found out that I was pregnant. I couldn't go to the Army because my family, we didn't believe in abortions. I couldn't do it. Anyway, I had got heavy pregnant, and Lady Z asked me to come over to her house. I went over there because her and this girl had gotten into it, and she and I was supposed to be together. We walked up to the front, and we were talking. I turn around, and a knife went in my face. All I kept seeing was this blade. I was seven months pregnant.

Lady Z was hitting her to get off me. I remember rolling out to the oncoming traffic. Some kind of way, they got her off me. The blood was in my eyes. They got me to the hospital, and I have four stitches inside and three out. I stayed in Texas for a little while, but I left. I was like,

"I can't do this anymore."

Ms. Millie let me stay at her house. My two boys and I stayed there until the pregnancy got full bloom. We stayed there as long as we could, and I ended up getting a job. I wanted my own place.

My first real place with my children was a garage with a concrete floor. It had a hole in the wall. I put up a big piece of tin, and I painted over that hole to make it like a home. When it was cold, it was cold. When it was hot, it was hot. That was in New Orleans. After that, I got involved with drugs.

I was shooting tees and blues, back then that's what they had. Quaaludes, whatever they had, drinking syrup. Whatever it was to get high, I was doing it.

I didn't feel like I was worth anything. I was infamous, not because of my addiction. My addiction was a symptom. I was trying to get away from all the other stuff that had gone on in my life.

When I was 7, my mom died. I went to stay with my grandmother and auntie. She loved me, but she had seven or eight kids of her own. I remember being outside playing. My dad drove up with this woman he had married, and he took my brother and didn't take me. I felt like something was wrong with me. Why didn't he want me? That's where it all begin. I wasn't good enough. So I started running away, started having sex, and started getting high. Why not? Who's going to care? These were great escape mechanisms. I thought that I was big and bad enough to do these things. Little did I know that I had a family that loved me.

By the time I made it to my 20s, I was struggling with my children in the streets. Pride wouldn't let me call my family. But had I called, my aunt would've taken them. I do believe that. So I go to the Department of Children and Family Services to see if they can help me. The lady said, "We can keep the kids for you until you get on your feet." I'm all for that, so they got my kids, and I tell them, "I'm going to leave you here for a little while so you can stay and go to school." DCFS slapped papers on me, saying it was neglect because I didn't have adequate housing. They never told me I was going to get a neglect charge. They said they were going to help me. I guess that was their way of helping me. I called my auntie and moved back to Chicago.

I cried every day. My auntie told me, "Bitch, stop crying." She didn't pull no punches. My children were gone. She told me we can't get anything done with me running on my emotions. "Shut up that crying. We gotta get these kids back."

DCFS told me I couldn't get the kids back until I got a place. We moved to a one-bedroom. They told me that wasn't big enough. Then they split my children up. My daughter was in one of those homes that I don't want her in. And my other children were in another suburb. Now I'm pissed. I can't do nothing about it.

So I get a larger apartment. The DCFS worker in Chicago saw that I now had a two-bedroom apartment. She reported that back to the workers in New Orleans, and they returned the two boys to me. So now I've got two boys, and my auntie, she said, "I'm proud of you. Now get the other one back." I said, "Yes, ma'am." She said, "You thought I was being cruel to you, but I was preparing you." I am very grateful for the way she talked to me, and to this day I appreciate that.

One day, I got a call, and the caseworker said, "Edwina, we're going to court today for your daughter. I'm going to recommend that she comes home with you." They don't know that I ain't got no money. I got to go to New Orleans to get my daughter. This lady I was taking care of, she said, "Edwina, I'm going to give you the money for your ticket. I'm going to pay you in advance, and you'll be back." I said, "Yes, ma'am, I'll be back."

She paid for my ticket. I went to New Orleans, first time flying in my life. I prayed the whole trip. The state of Louisiana bought my daughter's ticket. We got on that plane, and my daughter was talking. I said, "Girl, shut up and pray." I was scared. We got to Chicago, and we became a family again.

A lot of time passes. My children are all grown. They have their own children now. I started going back to church. I met a man named June. He turned me on to crack. I thought he had another woman, but I didn't know his other woman was a pipe. He took me to the crack house.

I had a choice. I often think about that. It wasn't that he put it in my mouth and made me smoke it. No. I should have known that something was wrong with that whole fucking picture. They were in the dark with candles lit everywhere like we were having a séance and people sitting on crates and ain't no lights on. I said, "Give me some of that." I had a choice. I asked to be fucked up. I did whatever it took to be wherever somebody said they loved me. I was searching for love in all the wrong places.

One night I gave him $100, and he came back with a piece. I said, "Damn, that's what you get for $100?" It just fit in my hand. Come to find out, he forgot the other piece in his hat. Now if you steal from me and I'm suppose to be your woman, that's when the happiness start going away. That's like stealing from your motherfucking self. People change when they smoke that shit.

I lied to my auntie. I called her up because we ran out of money. I said, "I've got to get some money. I've got to get a new tire that cost $100." Who doing tires at 1 a.m.? She said, "Come on and get it." And I went over there and got that $100. That was in November. By January, every-

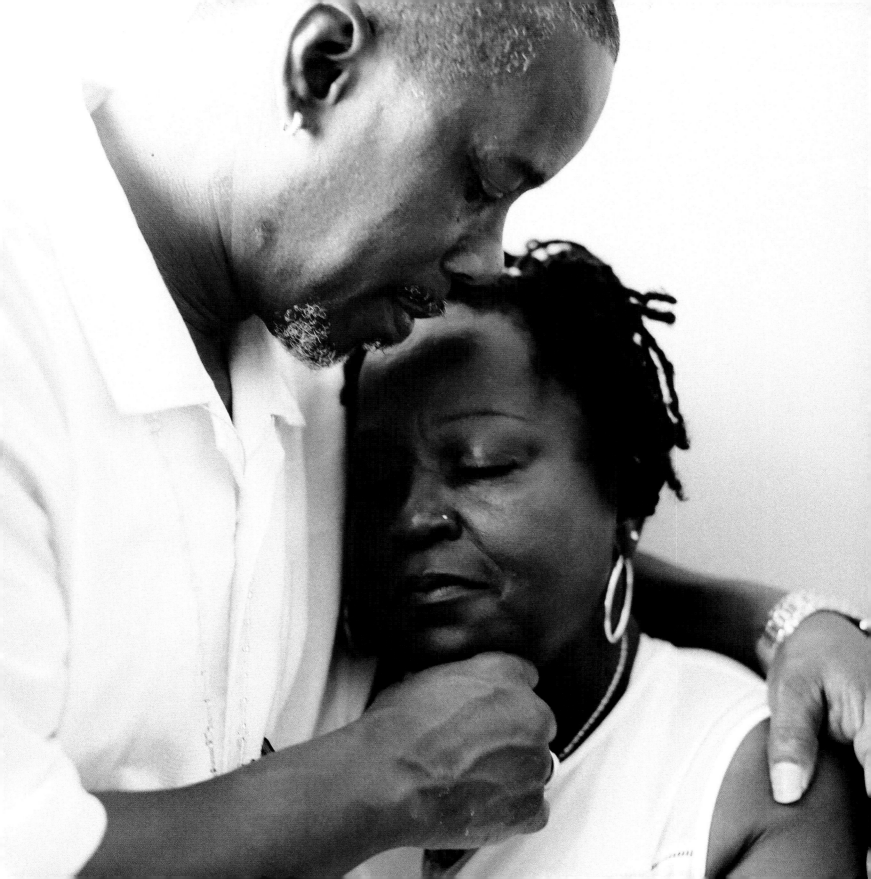

thing in my four bedrooms was gone. I was selling shit off the walls. I had nothing else to give. I had no more car. I had no more furniture to sell. I quit my job because getting high became more important than going to work. I also had my children trying to figure out what happened to their mom.

I ain't paid rent for five months. Now we got an eviction notice. I didn't care.

June said he was going out of town somewhere and that he'd be bringing drugs back. The truth was he was going to be a mule, and they were supposed to put him on a plane. He was supposed to fly. They ended up putting him on a Greyhound bus.

Illinois. Those people sent me to a place in Atlanta for a Christian-based recovery program. They took my Newports upon arrival, a whole carton of cigarettes. They told me I couldn't wear any pants, and I had to pray for breakfast, lunch, dinner. I asked them, "Why do we have to talk to Jesus that long before we eat?" They said, "We've got to repent for our sin." I said, "Oh no, this is some cult shit, I've got to get out of here." I called my son, and he sent me money for a bus ticket. I told them, "Give me my cigarettes and all my damn pants. Drop me off where you picked me up at."

I saw somebody at the bus station, and they knew where I could find crack. I traded in my ticket that my

I didn't feel like I was worth anything. I was infamous, not because of my addiction. My addiction was a symptom. I was trying to get away from all the other stuff that had gone on in my life.

Sunday morning I'm getting ready for church. I got the call from Atlanta police. They found him dead on the Greyhound bus. When they took him to the coroner, they found his body laced with cocaine—packs and packs and packs. All around his waist and legs. He was 34-years-old.

Now I'm out here by myself. I'm strung out. I'm on the street. I broke into my friend's house. She lived two blocks down. She had computers, TVs and stuff. I got all that shit. I was going to get high. My son said, "Mom, you need help." Police came to my house and asked me if I knew anything about it. The neighbor told the woman that I was at that house.

My son took me to the Potter's House in Maywood,

son sent, and was up in Atlanta, Georgia, in their projects, smoking, until the next day. And the next day, I called my son. He said, "Ma, I'm not sending any more money. Why didn't you get on that bus?"

Now I'm in Atlanta. They stole my luggage. I ain't got no clothes, walking around the bus station looking stupid. I met this guy. He worked at some big barbershop downtown. He never asked me for anything, no sex, no nothing. He said, "Baby, you need to go back home. I'm going to let you stay at this barbershop." Two days went by, and I called my son, and he paid for the ticket. That's how I got out of Atlanta.

When I got back to Maywood, I went back to the same old problem. I was just smoking. I didn't even eat, just smoking. And my son found me. My kidneys were hurting so bad because all I was doing was drugs and drinking alcohol. They took me to the county hospital. I got out of the hospital. I went right back doing the same things.

So one day I call my son. "I need money." He said, "Mama, meet me at the house. I'm on my way, and I'll give you your money." He comes there, him and his wife, and he took my car keys, talking about I ain't going nowhere. I jumped his ass. I went to beating him. He went downstairs to call the police. The police came. They took me to jail. I cried, "You want me to go to jail? After that, I was clean for two years.

Time passed, I ended up back on the streets of Chicago. I no longer wanted to even try to live anymore. That's when I met Mr. Freeman. He said, "Ma'am, what are you doing out here? You don't belong here." I said, "What you want?" He said, "I don't want nothing from you. A voice told me to stop and pick you up. Don't you have any people?" I started to cry. All I could remember was my baby son's phone number. Mr. Freeman let me use his phone to call my son. Mr. Freeman talked to my son. My son said, "I'm going to pay for a ticket. Put her on that bus. Do not let her tell you that she need to go back and get anything because she will be gone. Put her on the bus, please!" Mr. Freeman bought me a sandwich, got me a bottle of water. I was real dirty and funky. And he put me on that Greyhound bus. That's how I ended up in Madison, Wisconsin.

I stayed with my baby son. I called him the warden. He kept an eye on me like I was in jail. He knew he could not trust me. I ended up getting a place at Porchlight. I stayed clean for 22 months.

I was ready to go to the Gay Pride Parade in Chicago, but I stopped to go see my dad. I went to see him, and my dad looked at me and said, "I don't know what you come here for. I will never introduce you to my friends with that hair bald and red." He said I was a disgrace. All I wanted him to do was accept me and love me. Again, here I am, now a grown woman, and still not enough.

I jumped in my car and drove from Kankakee back through Chicago, got off at 63rd Street. I had stopped smoking for about a year, but I went to that gas station and bought a pack of cigarettes. It was the wrong place to be. I found somebody to get high with, and that was it. I gave him the money and my car keys to go get crack. The man never came back with the money or the car. Now I'm stuck in Chicago. I had to call my sponsor in Madison. They got me a Van Galder bus ticket. I got back here and told everybody that somebody carjacked me. I was lying, just lying. I believe they knew I was lying, too.

I would like to go back, just a little bit. Before I came to Madison, before I met Mr. Freeman, I was still doing the drugs. One day, a voice told me to go to the hospital. I drove to Madden Mental Health. I told the lady that I wanted to get some help. My eyes were bucked. I was sweating like I was in a sauna. I had become a human vacuum cleaner. Every time I saw a white speck, I'd pick it because I thought it was crack. I was tweeking. She listened to me. I wanted to get up to go smoke a cigarette. The lady said, "Well, you can't go out. We're going to keep you." I said, "Ms., I didn't ask you to stay. I wanted you to help me." What I was thinking, I don't know. They called the guards, and I wrestled with those guards, and they put me in a room. I guess it was my room.

When I did wake up, I'm looking at these people walking around this circle. Just walking around that little spot for hours. I said, "Ain't nothing wrong with me like these people. I need to get up out of here." She said, "Well, ma'am, all the things that you've done, the way you came in, if you try to contest, we will keep you here for the rest of your life. Yeah, I could just declare you legally insane." She had the pen and the power. They kept me there 59 days. They prescribed me some medicine. I didn't walk no circles. I just sat down and looked stupid. I was a smoker, and they explained in order for me to have smoking privileges, I had to be doing something, either work in the cafeteria or go to school. I chose school because I didn't have a GED.

When I went in the classroom, I was kind of slow with that medicine. I would just nod off. The lady said, "Why don't you challenge the test?" I said, "I don't know about that challenge." "Challenge the test, the GED test." Challenge was, as oppose to taking each subject, just go on and take the test. See where you are, because whatever you pass you won't have to take again. You just take the subjects that you struggled in. I said, "Well, okay." That lady let me take that test for three days because I was so slow. Lord and behold, I passed that test by two points.

I was very proud of myself that I got the GED. But I wasn't proud of the way I got it. When I tell people where I got my GED, they look at me. I was in the mental health place—psychiatric unit, as a matter of fact. When I first became addicted was November 26, 1999. The year that I got my GED was in 2000. I learned a lot about myself that year.

For example, I learned that when I'd first meet somebody, within the first 30 days or the first 60 days, I'd buy him a ring. Or I'd want to dress him. I didn't really get to know these men, but I'd shower them with things, hoping the more that I give them, the more they'd want to love me.

I wouldn't get love in return. I wasn't doing it for the right reason. I was doing it so that he could validate me, so that I could feel good about me. I needed for them to say that I was a good person. By me not getting that in return, I felt I was a failure. I used because I couldn't deal with that feeling. Why is it that I couldn't be enough? I believe they saw my insecurity. If you really knew the truth about me, would you still love me? I was always afraid of that. I either had to be a people pleaser so you could like me in some form, or put up a mask. I could put that mask on and be what I need to be for that moment.

I don't have to do that today. I'm a member of a 12-step program, and I do step work. I'm at a level where I struggle because I'm looking at some stuff that I don't like in myself. I will continue to fall short, and it's okay. I used to didn't feel that way. I never will arrive, and I accept that. But every day, I can do better than I did yesterday. If I make another mistake, it's okay.

I got these grown kids, three different men. What the hell, I'm a lesbian. This is wrong, crackhead. Who the hell wants me? Why would you? Who's going to marry me? I'm getting old. My biological clock is running out. Then I'm fat on all that.

I've never seen the beauty of what God had already made. I couldn't see the beauty of those trees because I was looking at the goddamn brown part, the part that was dying. I could never see the beauty of the whole picture that made me.

When I came to Madison, my son wouldn't tolerate no nonsense. I was angry with him because he didn't do like I think that he should've. He knew that somewhere in my program I was going to relapse because all I was thinking about was working, making money, getting clothes, get a car, getting a place.

A therapist told me that when you have issues and you don't deal with them, all it does is come back. Maybe a month, a year, they'll come back again. I didn't deal with none of that. I got all the materialistic things that I wanted, but I relapsed, after being clean those 22 months.

Now I'm going to tell you something. I never thought I was good enough to get anybody with any intelligence, so I liked sick-ass people. The sicker the fuck you were, the better I liked you.

So anyway, I'm working. I've got my job back at Belmont. I'm clocking checks. I put money in the bank. I'm in treatment, where I could just come and go overnight when I want. Well, I get in this relationship with this guy. I liked him because he was cool. I liked thugs. I liked a bad boy.

What happened was I'm going to work every day and this dude didn't have a job. So I bought him a watch, went to the mall, t-shirt, bought him a baseball cap, bought him chains. Oh girl, I was just dressing this bitch. I get back home one day back in the treatment place. And he got another girlfriend.

She lived there, too. I'm keeping him with packs of cigarettes, buying us cartons of cigarettes, so he never went around without cigarettes. Not knowing that this bitch is smoking the cigarettes that I bought. Now, there's another blow to my self-esteem. I had to leave there. End up going back with my son.

I ended up moving with somebody off Mill Street. I stayed there six months, went to my job. In six months, I made $20,000, and I smoked it all. I ended up leaving there and come back with my daughter-in-law. My job let me go, so I drew unemployment. Baby, they sent all those unemployment checks. Wrong move. I smoked that.

My brother calls, and that was in 2009. And he says, "Edwina, Dad is sick. He needs our help." "Really? Now he needs me, huh? I'm not coming." I got a job in Middleton at that nursing home. They were paying me $14 dollars an hour. "I'm not coming." My brother begged so.

I had got tired of being in Madison because I had blew everything. Sold phones, sold my daughter-in-law's bus tickets for the kids. They were scared to lay anything down around me. You know, you've got to sleep with your purse under your pillow.

I rented a U-Haul van. I loaded the little shit I had, and I drove that van all the way to Kankakee, Illinois. My point going down there was to find an easy place to stay, not to take care of my father. But I tell you this—when I got there, I wanted to tell him every fucking thing. He was laying in that bed, and he looked at me, and I had a look on my face. He looked at me, and he said, "Baby, whatever I've done to you, I'm so sorry." When he said that, my heart melted. I looked at him and said, "Damn, I can't even be mad now. I've got to forgive him, and let him go."

You see, my dad was an alcoholic, and he used to fight my mom. He took us to this house with a white picket fence. I'll never forget it. This man named Mr. Robinson with those shiny, funky-ass-looking pants and them fucking shoes. I must have been about 5. I would go in one room, my sister would be in another room, and I'm supposed to be taking a nap or something. That man would come and place himself between my legs and then all of a sudden, I'm wet. He would give my dad money in a bag.

And now we're here, taking care of my dad. All my life, I've taken care of old people, that's all I knew how to do, CNA work. I rolled my sleeves up, and I said, "Daddy, what we're going to do is never let you be dirty. We ain't going to have no bed sores. I'm here to take care of you." My brother stood there, and he cried. I cried. Daddy cried.

My brother painted that room. We put down new carpet. We hung Bible verses because he liked the Bible, put up new curtains, put his hospital bed in there. I got sheets that matched his t-shirts. He was color-coordinated. If I tell you them sheets were red, his shirts were red. If I change to navy blue, he's in blue. White, he was in white. Then I got those little wave caps because he was always complaining about his head being cold.

Me and my dad started building the relationship I always wanted. I would go in there, and he would say, "Oh, my wonderful, wonderful, daughter." These were the words I'd been wanting to hear all my life. He said, "I love you."

We had to give him his morphine. I clipped his toenails. His feet wasn't crudding at the bottom. We had the barber cut his hair in that bed. Hear me, what I'm saying? His fingernails stayed clean. He got where he couldn't go to the bathroom. He would tell us, these are his words —"It's coming up. It's coming up." We would run to put him on the toilet.

I remember when we turned on the music. He had a little diaper and his t-shirt, and I held him up, and we danced. He said, "I'm not going to be here for your wedding." That was way before I even thought about getting married. Man, I cried that day. He said, "I won't be here." Maybe a month or so after that, he started getting where he couldn't remember so much. In November, he died.

After my father passed, I came back to Madison by Thanksgiving. One day at work, I was pushing my med cart, because I passed meds. One guy put the light on to go to the bathroom. I went and put him on the toilet. My knee snapped. I fell, and so did he. He had to call for the nurses to get us both up. I went to the doctor, and the doctor said that I had to stop doing CNA work. That's all the work I'd ever done in my whole life. What was I going to do? I had to make a career change in my 50s.

My daughter-in-law had to buy my personal products. I felt less than a woman. She was paying for my cell phone and whatever else that I needed—deodorant, whatever. I applied for unemployment, but I didn't qualify because I stopped working because of a medical condition. So I applied for Social Security. I also applied for disability, and it didn't take long—three months—they gave me disability. That was a start, so I knew that I could take care of some stuff.

I went to a meeting and told my story. A lady there gave me a card and said, "Call me tomorrow." The card said CAC—Community Action Coalition. When I called, the lady said, "Well, I don't have anything for you, but I have a person you could talk to—Ms. Dee." Ms. Dee asked me to meet her on Cottage Grove, and God opened the doors. She brought me in, and I was like yeah, this is so nice, this is pretty. I saw myself in that apartment. I said, "I don't have any money." She dropped keys in my hand and said, "It's yours."

Girl, I just cried and ran all through the apartment. I didn't have a stitch of furniture to put in there. But somebody trusted me after all this long time, and baby, they brought all my little things. My daughter-in-law would try to give me little stuff like plants, something that I could use. All I had was all these bags.

Well, the next time I came back, Ms. Dee brought me some dishes, a microwave, glasses. And Ms. Dee, she called me and asked me did I need a bed because A1 Furniture was giving away beds, and they had a Memory Foam. She asked if I wanted it. I said, "Yes."

No more putting me out. No more telling me I gotta go. Lights were on. Man, everything just started growing from there. I know that things can happen. They did not happen because of things I've done. I didn't deserve any of that goodness. It was ONLY by GOD'S GRACE that I got it.

People say I talk about God too much. Y'all don't

know what He's done for me.

God has allowed me to go back to school. First, I graduated from Odyssey in 2011. Next, in 2012, I enrolled in Madison College.

I chose to be a substance abuse counselor. I chose that field because I've lived it. The books tell you that it takes this and it takes that, but they're not looking at the cause. They want to just put you into treatment. You should be clean immediately and that's that. A lot of things I didn't agree with. Sometimes you have to treat the cause.

I got into a huge debate with my instructors. They want to talk about what research says, and I was able to say, "Yes, I understand that. However, here's my experience." All these educators talked about these people, but they didn't consider my situation. You teach these black students how to write better prose. But when I go back home, and they're shooting over my head, those prose ain't doing nothing for me. Me being able to talk metaphorically is not going to help me.

My social change instructor taught me so much. What I really got from him was, "Okay, Edwina, you see all these situations? What are you going to do about it?" That stood out to me more than anything.

Don't get me wrong. I wanted a job that was prestigious. I'd like to achieve. But in my heart, I want to be in the trenches with the people. That's where I'm needed. I ain't needed way the fuck up there. They need somebody that will be right here with them. Be like a Harriet Tubman.

The job I have right now, today, has me in the trenches with the people. I am them. They are me. Tomorrow morning at 5 a.m., we're right there, together. I cannot look at them with my nose turned up as if I am better. It wasn't for the grace of God, there go I. That could be me. That would be me if I went back to that life.

Here in Madison, my eyes opened up to a lot of things. Our people are struggling, and we don't even know it.

My son told me something that I always remember: when your head is in the lion's mouth, you've got to work your way out, easy, because the lion will snatch it off.

If God brought me through, there's hope for you, too. What I'm putting out in the universe, it's like an invisible wall. Without God, I know I can't make it. My life shows me that it had to be a God that took care of me through all the stuff that I done been through. I'm still here.

Frank. He's my partner, my best friend. I could talk to him about any- and everything. He's encouraging. He knows me when I'm down, and sometimes I get mad because he'll tell me the truth. He will always be my sidekick, my lover, my man. Hey, he's all wrapped up in one big bundle. I love him to pieces.

I tell you, that day, when I walked up that aisle, I looked at him, and I kept on saying, "Is that for me?" It was a dream and the tears were flowing. I tried to keep from crying in front of people. When we locked arms, walking back from the pastor, it was a whole different world for me. I was no longer alone.

There's nothing uplifting this community. What needs to change? These are the people that have been forgotten. These boys stand out here, and half of them don't have an education. They've said we've come a long way. That used to burn me up in class. Well yeah, you guys have Martin Luther King Day.

Don't give up. Lost dreams do awaken.

We black women can recover from anything. But you've got to want to. That's the hit right there. You've gotta want it. And it ain't going to come overnight.

Wherever there's a blessing, there will be a battle. ❖

Yasmin

In the neighborhood where I matured into an adult addict, the main commodity was marijuana. If you were not linked to the right family, you could not open up shop. I was connected to a family with a matriarch named Reene. She was my other mother. Her children and I were close, and I used cocaine with all of the kids at one time or another. Her marijuana distribution operation was lucrative; she would buy the product and have her offspring sell it. Everyone had a day to work Monday through Sunday. Working. That's what we called it.

I was hanging out with Reene's oldest son, Barry. Barry was a gangster. I loved hanging out with him because he was big in the 'hood. Barry was feared and always had cocaine. I would give him the majority of my money so that I could be with him and use as often as he used. Needless to say, Barry would disappear sometimes and leave me to get my hustle on. I learned fast how to do that. I moved through the block like I didn't have a family down the street. I had a young son that was being raised by my mother, but I was beginning to spiral out of control.

One incident from that time stands out. My sister was getting on my case. "Come home and buy your son some shoes." "Fuck you, you buy them. You're so concerned about him, you buy 'em." Back then I was still working. My life had not completely fallen apart. I could go to work, and I could go to school, but I wanted to hang out and be part of the family. I went to Chicago City Colleges where, if you were 18, you can work on degree classes while you're working towards your GED. I managed to get 54 credits that came to Madison with me. I never got my GED in Chicago.

You remember Sitel? Everybody who was anybody was working at Sitel. It was a call center out in Middleton. It went out of business. They hired me to work on the Prudential Insurance contract, and then when they saw I didn't have a GED, they said, "Oh, we can't offer you this job." So I went on to take my GED. Every day they gave a test at MATC. I took it, got it in like five days, and I went back out there with proof that I had my GED. They gave me the job. I only kept it six months because some man that called in on the contract that I was working on sounded good on the phone. I gave him my phone number, and I lost my job because of that. Just nuts. Crazy.

When I came from Chicago, I was still 'hood. I was instructed to call a number to get into a shelter. I invented a story to get into the one for battered women, thinking that I could get permanent housing faster. I said that my man from Chicago had followed me here and was after me. He had run me out of Chicago, and now he was in Madison. I was scared for my life. The call center didn't fall for that shit. "You can go to the women's shelter at the Salvation Army." "Damn," I thought. "It worked in Minnesota." To the women's shelter I went.

I don't know if you know about the single women's

shelter at the Salvation Army. They've got these beds that look like Murphy beds. You know what a Murphy bed is? The ones that come out the wall back in the old days. They had the beds that blend in with the wall, and you pull the bed down and make it up. First night there, I took a shower, put my stuff in a locker. No lock, but I had nothing to lock up because I came to Madison with just the clothes on my back. After that night, I woke up and was told to meet with this woman named Monu. She was East Indian. She asked me, "When you called, you said you were on drugs. Well, do you want to get off them?" I was like, "Not particularly." I told her that I hadn't used in the week that I had been in Madison. I remember after a few days here my daughter-in-law was driving me to

I didn't connect the dots right at that time, but looking back, God set me up for a lot of things that happened.

So, Monu called Hope Haven. When I got to my son's house, they called me. That doesn't happen. I have worked for Hope Haven since then, and they tell you to call their number every day until they can find you a bed. When I called them back, they asked, "Are you serious and ready for treatment?" I said, "Yeah." They said, "Okay, be here Monday." I stayed in treatment for six weeks. I was beginning to like what I was hearing. I was being educated about my brain on drugs and stuff like that. I was getting it like I hadn't gotten it before. I started going to meetings.

I met this woman, LeAnna. I asked her if she would

I needed to feel like I had some protection, like somebody loved me and cared enough about me to do something and not just turn a blind eye to that.

MOM (Middleton Outreach Ministries) to get me some clothes, and I felt something in my jacket pocket. It was my crack pipe. I called it my Uzi. I rolled the window down. I threw that thing out the window, and I don't know where I was when I did it. That was the end of that.

God is good. He just lifted from me the desire to use. I hadn't been to a meeting. I wasn't in treatment, but I still hadn't used. I had no money, but an addict don't need no money to get high, and that's for damned sure. So I met with Monu. She asked me again about the drugs. I said I wasn't necessarily thinking about not ever using again for the rest of my life. I wasn't—although I had prayed that prayer and wrote it down, and I've got it somewhere in my stuff back in Chicago, where I had asked God to begin the process of making me drug-free for the rest of my life. I put it in the 23rd Psalm in a Bible at my momma's house.

be my sponsor. Long story short, LeAnna took me under her wing. She used to compare our lives when I would read my step work to her. She'd say things like, "It's amazing how parallel our lives are." She was a poor little rich white girl from Texas. I'm a black girl from the inner city streets of Chicago, ain't got shit. And she would say, "We're alike." After knowing LeAnna for about two years, she bought a house in Janesville and she asked me if I would like to be her roommate. But I didn't have a job and I didn't drive, so how in the hell am I going to get back and forth, you know, from her house to a job? She accepted me just as I was, which meant a lot to me.

I'm still in treatment during this time, and I didn't have anything, no job, no money, no clothes. In order to have underwear, pajamas, or anything else that I wanted, I used to leave Hope Haven on passes. I would catch a bus to West Towne Mall and shop like I was spending money. I would go through them stores and find the things that I wanted, to make myself feel better. I would come home with pretty panties, a watch, earrings, satiny pajamas. One day when I did that, this feeling came over me like I had just took a hit of crack, and it scared me. It scared me bad.

By now I'm going to church on the regular, and I have a relationship with my pastor and his wife. I told my pastor what I did and how it made me feel. He told me to take the stuff back to the store. I told my sponsor. My sponsor said, "Don't you take that stuff back." She said, "Yasmin, if they see you putting it back they're going to think you've taken it, and they could arrest you for shoplifting. Give it away. Don't sell it for profit, just give it away." So I gave a few people a few things.

Next amazing thing that happened was when I met Jan Miyasaki. Jan became my case manager and my mentor. Jan directed me to go to outpatient treatment at ARC Community Services. I went through that program. After I graduated from there, that's when I got the job at Sitel. After I left Sitel, I had a hard time finding work. I had a felony drug conviction on my record from 1995. Again, my hustle abilities came into play, and I used a made-up work background. I was contacted by UW Continuing Education. They have a program called Wisconsin Women Education Network (WWEN). And they asked me to tell my story. They had me on the front cover of their magazine, *Putting the Face to Recovery*. This opportunity ignited a spark that led me to hang out at the South Branch Library. It was there that I found an application to the Odyssey Project, a University of Wisconsin-Madison humanities class for adult students facing economic barriers to college. I applied for and was accepted into the 2006-2007 class. It was at this time that the 54 cred-

its that I earned at Richard J. Daley and Kennedy-King, two of the Chicago City Colleges, came into play. I had great support between LeAnna, Jan, Emily Auerbach, Odyssey's director, and my recovery family. During this time I had even began to earn the love and support of my siblings and son.

As I reflect back on my life, things could have been really different. In 1983, I met this guy. I think he was 23 and I was 27, or something like that. He lived two doors from me, and we became a couple. Girl, it looked like his body had been chiseled from marble. I called him Stallion. Stallion and I was together for four years. To the public, we looked like the perfect couple. He was real attractive, and all the girls loved to flirt with him. But when we'd go home and close the door, he'd beat the shit out of me. Even though I used before I met Stallion, being in this abusive relationship caused my addiction to take off.

I already had a son. I got pregnant at 21. I was really torn because I wanted to abort. Abortions had just become legal. I was young and I was living pretty good. I felt like if I didn't have the baby, I may never get pregnant again. I may never have another opportunity to do this. So I brought my son in the world, and I don't regret it. But when he was four months old I was pregnant again. His daddy was in Germany. We hadn't had sex since October, so he couldn't be the father. This time I wasn't confused. I knew what I had to do.

I decided I was going to the county and have an abortion. Well, I ran into my momma on the bus with her nosy ass, and she started giving me the stink eye and trying to put a hex on me. All that old bullshit. And I was like, listen, I'm not going to bring something in the world that I don't want. That would not be fair to the kid or me. And Lord knows I didn't want this baby. I was just careless. That was in 78. Well, in 80, I was pregnant again, and I did the same thing again. After two unwanted pregnancies, I got my tubes tied. I like to party, and that was more important to me at the time than being a parent. Ain't that a bitch? Little did I know I was going to meet a young maniac without children. Whenever he thought about me not being able to give him a baby, he would beat me. I accepted the abuse when he told me he loved me, and the sex was the bomb, so it was easy to keep going back.

Stallion and me would be fighting all night. We was calling the police on each other. His mother told him, "I will buy you a ticket anywhere in the world one-way, to get your ass away from her." So eventually she bought him a ticket to LA. After Stallion left my life, I was evict-

them, "Fuck this. You ain't helping me. I'm giving you everything. You ain't giving me nothing, so I won't be back."

I was destined to be an addict. I started drinking when I was 8. My mother used to have these parties at home. We're talking in the early 60s. You know, love, peace and hair grease, right? My mother was in her early 40s. She was still beautiful, and she liked to have a good time. The only problem was the man she fell in love with, who became my little sister's father, was sexually molesting me from the time my mother brought him into the home. I was 3.

My mother was born in 1924 in rural Mississippi, an only child. She had uncles. There were lots of men around. And she looked like a white girl. So I bet you

I remember walking into a mental health clinic. When asked why I was there, I just started telling my story about being in love with a man who was beating the shit out of me, and I couldn't stay away from him, so I knew I had to be crazy.

ed from my apartment. The landlord was a slumlord anyway; I didn't give a fuck. I didn't pay rent for six months; my addiction was full-blown. When he told me he was going to evict me, I just waited the process out. He went to court; I didn't.

Shit was so crazy in my life back then, I even tried therapy. I remember walking into a mental health clinic. When asked why I was there, I just started telling my story about being in love with a man who was beating the shit out of me, and I couldn't stay away from him, so I knew I had to be crazy. She invited me to come back and talk to a therapist, which I did. This went on for a few weeks until I went in there drunk as hell. I was tired of talking. I wanted help. So I went in there, and I told

dollars to doughnuts that my mother was molested. She handled it. She figured if I can handle it, you can handle it. Just shut up and keep moving. But I couldn't handle it. I needed to feel like I had some protection, like somebody loved me and cared enough about me to do something and not just turn a blind eye to that.

So at these parties, I would be called in to dance. The men there were relatives and close friends, and they would pass me around from lap to lap after the dance was over. I didn't know that anything was wrong when they would slip their fingers inside my panties. Everybody was drinking, and nobody was paying attention to what was going on with me. My mother was loose at the time and loved to drink and party, baby.

I found out that I liked to drink and party, too, at the age of 8. I would wake up many times after one of those parties on top of the chifferobe because I'd drunk a whole beer. I'm 8-years-old, and I was drinking to the point of passing out. By the time I was 10, I was still drinking. I never stopped drinking. Now I'm smoking, too. My friend, Loretta, her mother worked during the day. During the summer months, we would sit in the kitchen at her house smoking cigarettes with cold cans of beer, like adults. I wasn't even in fifth grade, and we was living like that.

Childhood wasn't bad, or I didn't see it as bad. I didn't even know that what was happening to me was bad; not yet. The older my mother got, the more of a matriarch she became in the community. My mom and dad separated in 1952 after the fifth child. But they continued to mate and made three more babies. Baby number nine was by another man.

In the late 50s and early 60s, young girls didn't go to their mothers and tell them your boyfriend is coming in my bedroom at night. Well, hell, I'm 3, 5, 7... I don't have those words anyway. As a result, I grew into a rebel-

lious teenager. I went from being an honors student to a drunk and later a crackhead. I argued and fought with my mother constantly, not physically but verbally.

Things got so bad between us that she had to call in the cavalry. I had an older brother at the time, Junior, my mother's firstborn. He came whenever she called. One day, he pulled up in front of the house, and he said, "Get in the car." As soon as I got in, I just burst out in tears because I didn't know what he was going to do to me. He was pissed off because I was messing with his momma. He took me around the block, and he pulled over, and he was telling me, "If this is what you choose to do with your life, that's your choice. Keep that shit away from my momma house." I was in my mid-20s. My using was out of control. I didn't see a way to come back from being so far out there. I hadn't gotten into really selling my body. I was what they call a nonprofit whore at the time. I was just having fun. My use escalated, and my relationship never got better with my mother, even until the day she died.

I used to say I'm addicted to dick and dope. My family thought it was a joke. My mother used to say, "By the time you know what that pussy worth, it ain't gonna be worth shit." And I used to tell her, "I'm not gonna be a whore like you want me to be." I wanted to be a madam. I was enjoying myself. I did it when I wanted to do it. I was living in my mother's house with my boyfriend. I wasn't happy with that situation. When I finally got rid of him, he left me with no windows in the dead of winter. I started having parties at the house, renting rooms for the night like it was a motel, letting the dope boys do their thing. Sometimes I'd have big spenders at my house. They would always want more girls to party. Once the girls got there, I would tell them to go into my room and put on sexy lingerie. We would sit at the table with the men, you know, legs wide open in these sexy outfits. I had a glass top table that the men could see through while we were getting high.

I considered it a successful night if I could get high all night and not perform a sexual act. All I wanted to do was get high all day and all night, every day and every night. Nobody expected me to be responsible for shit because I was a crackhead. I had no responsibilities. After a few years of partying at momma's house, I started neglecting paying the bills. Of course this led to me leaving, but not before writing a letter to God. In the letter, I petitioned Him to begin the process of making me drug-free for the rest of my life. Within the year, my son came to Chicago, found me where I was, and brought me to Madison, Wisconsin. The rest is history.

I am 60 years old. I've got scars that only plastic surgery can take off me. I've been smacked upside the head and punched in the mouth. I haven't had a man physically abuse me since 2003, by the grace of God.

You know, God came into the world, Jesus came into the world so that you may have life and have it more abundantly, right? And that's what I get, because I surrendered. I said, "Lord, whatever you want to do, I say yes. I'm going to be obedient." He was walking with me all along. He's been in my ear saying, "Would you please stop, and let me love you?" And I'd be like, "I know you love me, but right now I want to have sex, and I can't have sex with you."

When I finally was so beat down by the street and the lifestyle, I stepped over the threshold and there He was with his arms open. He just took me in and cuddled me and held me and said, "Now I can show you what real love is."

I come from a dysfunctional, messed-up family. I think that's a ministry for me. I do believe that my life is being shaped for ministry.

Girl, and I love Jesus. I love to drink. I love to party. But God has delivered me from it. I thank Him so much. I did the footwork but He set the path. And He's still out here. And so, you know, to whom much is given much is required, right? And it's like, oh my God, what I do I gotta do?

What the devil meant for evil, God turned it around for my good. My experience in the street has helped me to earn a bachelor's of science, and I am candidate for a master's in social work from one of the top schools in the country, the University of Wisconsin-Madison. As grimy as my lifestyle was twelve years, one month and five days ago makes it so much sweeter to have the lifestyle I have today. Today, I am a professional that helps people find the light in their lives. As a clinical substance abuse counselor, I strive on a daily basis to help people find their way out of the proverbial cave. ✽

Sheila

I am a recovering addict, and I have 29 years clean. In recovery, I make 12-step meetings. A part of the meetings is giving back that which was so freely given to me. Sharing my experiences, strengths, and hopes with other people shows them that they, too, can stop using drugs and find a new way of life. I must be accountable.

There are times when I am called upon, within Narcotics Anonymous meetings, to share with whoever's in the meeting my experiences, strengths, and hopes. I've never ever, ever, ever, ever liked to share, and I cringe at the thought of doing so. I do it because I must. I must give back, but I don't relish it. This is part of being accountable. I stand on the shoulders of those who came before me. I must be accountable.

I was a problem child. I was the oldest of three and the only girl. I got pregnant at 15. My mother, wanting more for me than she had for herself, got me an abortion that I ended up paying for because I had a part-time job. I lived in a strict household. I wasn't allowed to do anything, or so I thought at the time. She was always on my case because I was a girl. My two younger brothers were allowed more freedom than me because they were boys. That was very unfair. So I felt like I was searching for something. I didn't know what I was searching for, but I was searching.

When I got pregnant again, I was a freshman in college. I dropped out and got married. I was 19, and went from my mother's house to a marriage. I did not want a girl. I wanted a boy, because I knew the hard time I had given my mother in raising me, and I didn't want the same for myself.

I wanted a boy, and I got a boy. I loved my son, but I was not at all ready for motherhood. Not at all. I had not a clue.

My husband and I separated often because he would jump on me, and I couldn't beat him, so I would leave only to go back repeatedly. We separated for two years, and in that time span he moved to Michigan and I stayed in Illinois. I began a series of one-night stands. I would go into bars and sit at the bar, order a drink—I didn't drink, didn't know anything about drinking—and I'd let a man buy me a drink and then take me to a hotel. Later in life, I realized I was looking for love in all the wrong places. I needed to be wanted. I needed to be needed. Two years, that's a long time. That's a lot of one-night stands.

I reunited with my husband, and I moved to Pontiac, Michigan. That lasted maybe nine months. We started fighting again, and I left for good. I moved to Detroit. Once I separated from my husband—oh, immediately, the first week—I slept with his first cousin. I don't know why; I was not really attracted to him. It just happened. I think I needed to be wanted, part of the elusive, ever-present search. That destroyed any relationship that my husband would have had with his son.

I was not at all prepared to be a mother. I would buy clothes. I'd take him and everybody in the neighborhood—all his cousins—and we'd go to museums and to zoos, and we'd do a bunch of wonderful things, but I didn't have time to be a mother. I didn't want to take time to be a mother.

My son cried out for help, and I chose to ignore it or just didn't know that it was a cry for help. People told me it was a cry for help, so I can't say I didn't know. In school, he would be really disruptive. They had parent-teacher conferences. I'd go. And they suggested that I get him some help. I got him help. I took him to see a psychiatrist, and they suggested that I might also need help, that I was the problem.

At some point, I began using drugs. I started out smoking reefer. I didn't hide it, and that was an issue

to court for something—I don't remember what—and the judge said to me: "It definitely looks like you cannot control your son. If you can't control him, we can." He said, "I'm going to give you a continuance so you can think about whether you can handle him." He said, "If you can't, you come back and tell me, and we'll keep him for 30 days, which will teach him a lesson." All I could think was that he would be gone for 30 days, and I would be able to get high uninterrupted. His court date was two weeks before his 14th birthday. He didn't know, but I knew, that when we went back to court I was going to tell the judge I couldn't handle him so I could have a 30-day vacation. When I did that, they kept him. The look on his face broke my heart. But I didn't stop it. I didn't

I needed to learn how to be a mother to a son that was grown. And how do you do that? That was extremely hard for me. But I did it with the help of countless other women. I redefined who I was.

for my son. In school they were teaching "just say no to drugs" and here is his mama doing drugs, and he's worried that I would die or go to jail. But I didn't see that. I didn't want to see that.

His problems in school got to be worse and worse, and the police got involved. They put him in this special education program and suggested that he take Ritalin. When I gave it to him, he was a different person, like a zombie. And I couldn't do that. I wouldn't do it. I stopped giving it to him. Later, I would often wonder if I had kept giving it to him, would it have helped him? I don't know. But I didn't.

My drug use progressed to the point where mothering interfered with my getting high. My son had to go

change my mind. I didn't ask the court to give me another chance. I allowed them to take him. His behavior once he was incarcerated in St. Charles escalated, so that 30 days turned into 18 months, which began a life of institutionalization. He's been in and out of jail ever since. He is now 46 and is currently in jail.

Infamous? Yeah, I'm an infamous mother. I love my son to death. It's because of who I am that he is who he is. He didn't have a chance because I didn't give him a chance.

I've begun to make amends to those people, places, and things that I harmed throughout my life. It took me a long time to be able to stop feeling overwhelmed with the shame and the guilt. Once I got clean and stopped using and the fog lifted, I was able to look at me and where I came from, all the things that I did, with a different perspective, taking ownership of everything that was mine, rightfully mine. I tried living a different life so as not to repeat those things.

My first and hardest project was making amends with my son. I needed to make amends with him. Saying "I'm sorry" was not enough because I could and did say that with ease. I could say I'm sorry all day long. I needed to be there for him. I needed to learn how to be a mother to a son that was grown. And how do you do that? That was extremely hard for me. But I did it with the help of countless other women. I redefined who I was. First off, I accepted things about me that I didn't like in order to change them. Making amends with my son is a lifelong process. I continue to do that to this day. And what it looks like now is much different from what it looked like 28 years ago, when I first got clean. Today, I can offer unconditional love, tough love, and compassion. Now, I know more about what it means to be a mother.

I've helped other women who found themselves in similar circumstances, using or being used. I've shown them that there's a different way. I've shown them how to begin to love themselves. My behavior, a great deal of my life, was a result of me not loving me. I had to learn how to love myself so that I could begin to love others. I am able to do this because other women showed me how. This is another part of giving back that which was so freely given to me.

I've been through some health challenges. I smoked for over 40 years, and as a result, I had lung and kidney cancer. I'm a survivor of both. I had no treatment other than surgery for the lung cancer. For the kidney cancer, I had surgery and Rituxan, which got rid of the rest of the disease.

I have become a mentor for people who have cancer, any kind of cancer. I'm currently mentoring this elderly white man. He is 72, and he has lung cancer and is afraid. I get a lot of satisfaction out of mentoring, and I have to say that I not only mentor people who have had cancer but people who struggle with drug abuse.

I've always felt as though I did not have a creative bone in my body. There were people who could draw, who could sew, who could play instruments. They had all these talents. I do water aerobics three days a week. One day, as I was leaving water aerobics, I passed by this great big room, and there was a roomful of women and sewing machines. I stuck my head in the door and somebody said, "Come on in." I did. They told me that they were quilting, and they showed me what they were doing. Then the educational chairperson came in and told me they were going to be ending for the summer. She said, "If you come back by June 16th, I will have a supply list for you, and you'll have all summer to get the supplies. Then come back September 2nd."

I came back, and I have been quilting ever since. I love it. I absolutely, positively love it. I had to face my fear that I could not do this or that I was doing it wrong or that I was making mistakes. It's a learning experience. I absolutely, positively love it. I do have talents!

I got involved in this group called Gone But Not Forgotten. It's an organization that honors black men who have been killed by police. They had pictures and stories of the men. You create a square with this person's name and their date of birth and date of death, and sometimes the circumstances of their death. That was so cathartic. I can't even explain the feeling I got when I sewed a person's name. We came together and talked about what it was like, what we felt. It was wonderful, absolutely wonderful.

I have gotten involved in other quilting guilds and quilting projects because, yes, I love quilting. I have not found anyone in my family who quilted. Most people say, "My grandmother, my-great-grandmother quilted." I don't have that. My mother has a quilt that is made out of wool, and I remember it because it is very heavy. When I asked about it, she told me that she received it because she was a young mother and on public assistance. There were social service organizations that helped young families. We were adopted by such an agency. They took the kids to the show or to the museums. They did social activities with them. She received this quilt from such an agency. She has it to this day.

My mother got sick in her sophomore year in high school. Her grandmother thought she was pregnant. They took her to the doctor and found that she had tuberculosis. She was 16. In those days, they quarantined you, so she was put in a sanatorium and had to quit school. She met my father, who was also quarantined. Unbeknownst to my mother, he was married with a family.

I was born in a sanatorium. I only stayed two weeks because they were afraid I would catch tuberculosis. My great-grandmother wanted my mother to put me up for adoption. She refused. Because I could catch TB, I was placed in a foster home where I stayed for the first five years of my life. I was reunited with my mother. Because she did not finish high school, when she was discharged, not having a skill or diploma, we were on public aid.

After I left the TB sanatorium at two weeks old, I did not see my father again until I was 50. My whole life, I looked and searched for him. My mother told me that my brother underneath me had the same father. Mother said she maintained a relationship with him from day one that she was in there until after she came out in '53. She got on public aid, and public aid went after him for child support. He was a cab driver. He quit his job at that cab company. My mother had a relationship with his mother, and his mother told her not to come around anymore.

I wanted my father. I needed my father. That is what the two years of one-night stands were about. This need for a father teaching me things, loving me, was a part of the reason I could not be a mother to my son.

In spite of that, and because of that, I consider myself to be a phenomenal woman today. I did not always believe this about myself. My self-esteem was virtually nonexistent. But today I know who I am, and I love who I am. I am a grandmother of a 5-year-old. He is a joy.

I did ten years of therapy where I went back and reparented my inner child. I went through this rebirthing of me and giving my inner child what she needed, what she didn't get but still needed. I got to understand why I made the decisions that I made. By understanding and owning and reshaping that, and by reforming and rebuilding and remodeling me, I'm a much different person than I was.

I had cancer twice. I had a hysterectomy. I had 11-plus abortions. Talk about low self-esteem and infamous mothers. God... So much of my life that was negative and positive... all of that, all of that faith, all of that is in the fiber of my being. All of that is me. All of that is me.

I couldn't afford to roll over and play dead. That's not who I am. That's not who I was. I wanted to run and hide. Using was about not feeling. That was the purpose of using. I no longer have to do that. I'm free.

I tried suicide once in my life. I was seven months pregnant. I had gone to the doctor in May, and he told me that my baby would be born any day now. I came home excited because I was tired of being pregnant, and told my husband, and he told his mother, and being the woman that she is, she said, "Any day? But that means you're not the father, because that means she's nine months pregnant." He is the father! I know who I went to bed with. First, he called the doctor. Then his mother called. Then his sister called. And the doctor stopped taking calls. I had all these people against me, looking at me with disgust. Well, I took whatever was in the medicine cabinet, trying to kill myself. I was rushed to the hospital on Memorial Day. My doctor apologized to me and said that he told my mother that the baby would be here when it got here. My son was born in July.

I'm able to look at other women and feel empathy and not judge, because but for the grace of God there go I, and I've been there in some instances. I have not always been able to not be judgmental. I could look at you and decide I did not like you. I had to work real hard to overcome that, to not look down my nose at you, and that was just because I wasn't accepting me. I didn't accept who I was, so I definitely couldn't accept who you were.

A superpower that I have is I would help anybody. I'm a helping soul. My friends have said that I would let anyone stay with me, would help anyone if it was within my power. That superpower comes from my mother. I am who I am because I am my mother's daughter. As a child living in Englewood, I watched my mother fix hot, steaming thermos of coffee for the firemen in the dead of a Chicago winter. The coffee would curdle when she added milk or cream. She cried because she could not help them unless it was without cream. Who does this? My mother.

For years, my relationship with my mother was a tumultuous one. She could reduce me to tears with the bat of an eye. And I've worked real hard to grow up in my eyesight—not hers, in my eyesight—and I think I'm most proud of that. I'm most proud of the relationship that I now have with her.

I bought a two-flat building, gutted and rehabbed it, and I convinced my mother to sell her house and take the first floor. As a result of us living together, our relationship has gotten so much better. But I went through hell and high water because, as I say, she can reduce me to tears just with a look. But once I grew up in my eyes— once I grew up—I was able to accept truths I couldn't accept before. I gained self-esteem.

In January of 2017, my mother made her transition. After her homegoing plans were finalized, I got her two phone books and began calling people with the information. They, someone from her church, called me to say that she had received calls from church members saying someone had called them. She wanted to know if I knew anything about that. I told her that I had taken my mother's two phone books and began calling people. She informed me that I was calling church members. Well, I didn't know who was a member and who wasn't, I just knew that people that my mother knew needed to know that she made her transition. She asked me, "Who does that?" I do, because my mother did. It must be another superpower we share. I miss her dearly. God has allowed me to be able to say that I have been the best daughter that I could be once I stopped using drugs. She is now an ancestor. ✤

Mistee

I am a single African American mother of two children who have two different fathers, and I don't have a typical 9-to-5 job to support my family.

I have one child whose father is a little more hands-on than the other. I don't want that to cause any jealousy between them, and I want to instill in them how important love is in families. Even though we can't pick our blood, we have to respect who we share it with.

I don't get support from my children's fathers, but I don't talk down about them to my girls. I'm not lacking support, either.

For the last three years, I do what I call "pay it forward." I either go into a grocery store and purchase someone's groceries randomly, or if I'm out at a restaurant or something, I pay for someone's food. I choose food because it's something we need to live.

I went to this restaurant with my mom, her boyfriend, and my children. It's called Five Loaves. And there was a couple next to us, a husband and wife, and we all ended up interacting and talking and just having a good time.

When the bill came, I paid for everyone's meal, including the couple that was sitting next to me. And the husband was like, "You don't have to pay my bill. We have money. It's okay. I can do that." And I say to them, "No, I want to do it. I enjoyed you all's company, and I want you just to pay it forward. Do something nice for someone else." And he says, "Wow. Okay, I'm going to do that."

I ended up going back to the same restaurant—this is a couple of months later—and this man walks up to me and gives me $40. And I ask, "What is this for?" He says, "You don't remember me?" And I say, "No." And then he says, "My wife and I were here a few months ago, and you bought our food." And I was like, "Yeah, I remember. Okay, how you doing?" And he says, "You told me to pay it forward, and I hadn't done it, so I'm paying it forward back to you. So here's $40 for your meal." And I was like, "Wow, I appreciate that, thanks."

There was another man sitting next to me, and we were having small talk. And he asked, "What was that about?" So I explained to him that I randomly pick people and buy their food, whether it's at a grocery store or at a restaurant. And he said, "Wow, I've heard of people doing stuff like that, but I've never met anyone."

We talked a little longer, and he got called to his table, because we were in a waiting area. He went to eat, and eventually I got called. So at the end of my meal with my daughter, I asked the waitress for a to-go bag and my check. She said, "Well, that man you were talking to earlier, he paid for your bill,"—which was the guy that I was telling about the pay-it-forward thing. He covered my bill, and I had $40 from the guy earlier.

I believe that people should just live their life in gratitude and give. I'm a believer in giving and not holding on, because when you hold on to something, you don't allow something else to come in.

I have a cousin, and she needed to go to the doctor. I took her. During her appointment, my daughter and I waited in the car. My baby says, "Mommy, I'm hungry." I tell her, "Okay, well, we can get something to eat." I thought about going to McDonald's because it was cheap and fast, but I really wanted to sit down and have something good. So we end up going to a sit-in restaurant.

We're at the table. My 2-year-old wants to learn how to use a fork and cut with a knife. I'm teaching her. A man comes up to me, he says, "I've been watching you and your daughter, and she's really intelligent. You're doing a great job with her." I say, "Thank you, sir."

Now, mind you, before we went to the restaurant, I was having a conversation with God saying: "I know I can't afford this restaurant right now because I've got other things that I need to do. But I know you're going to make a way. And I know my daughter and I want to come here and enjoy ourselves, and I'm not going to stress over the lack."

The man gives me a $10 bill, and I say, "Wow, thank you, sir." But in my mind I'm saying, "Hey, this $10 is going to go towards my meal. Isn't it great?"

So my daughter and I are still interacting with one another. The waitress comes, takes our order. He comes back over to the table; he gives me a $20 bill. And I looked at him; I was like, "Wow, what is this for?" And he says, "I don't know. Just take it." "Thank you. I really appreciate it." And now I have $30—

I know I'll be able to pay for it now.

He goes back to his seat. My daughter and I are still doing our thing. And then the man gets up and comes back to the table and gives me another $20. By this time, my eyes are filling up with tears because I know that I don't have the money that I needed for this, but now I have the money to pay for my bill and $20. That's gas money right there.

So my eyes are filling up, and I was like, "Thank you." I'm like, "I don't understand why you're doing this, but thank you."

There was a guy across the table from me, and he says, "Well, at least you didn't have to do anything for it." And everybody in the restaurant is looking at me now, like wow, what's really going on?

So our food comes. I look over at the guy; he's ordering his food. My daughter and I are eating our food. And he comes back over to the table again, and he hands me another $20. Now the tears are coming down my face big-time, and I'm like, "Thank you. Whatever's putting this on your spirit and your heart, I just want to say thank you. I don't want to block your blessings by telling you no or 'take it back,' but I just want to say thank you."

So he goes and sits back down. His food comes; he's eating his food. We finish eating. The waitress comes over. I ask her for a to-go bag. And she gives it to me, and I say, "Can I get my bill?" She says, "That man paid your bill."

So by this time I have $70, and my bill is paid, and I'm just in the restaurant thinking back continuously and crying.

Well, I get our stuff together, and I walk past him; I was like, "Sir, I don't know what to say except thank you. I can't think of anything else. Just to say thank you." Then he gives me another $20. He's like, "This is for the road."

I walk out of that place with $90 in my pocket and our meal paid for from a complete stranger. And that's why I always pay it forward, because it's going to come back. Karma is real. And that's it.

I am who I am today because I have gone through many of life and many of its experiences without holding any grudges.

Okay, here's an example: my oldest daughter's father.

In the beginning, he was a hands-on dad, but then he met a young lady that already had five children, and they got together, and he Xed my daughter completely out of his life.

To go from seeing her dad the first six years of her life—like seeing him all the time, every day—to not seeing him at all for two years was really hard on my daughter. I watched her cry. I watched her be sad. I watched her fault herself. And I had to keep talking her through it. And at one point, I got angry with him—really angry with him—because even though my daughter would call him crying, it wasn't enough for him to do something different. It's like it just went through one ear and out the other.

psyche, because you now know abandonment. He grew up knowing abandonment from his dad, so it shouldn't surprise me that he was able to turn his back on his child and abandon her, because that's what he's experienced his whole life. He's never had anyone to identify with when it comes to being a father and being a man and having the experience of being a child. He never had that.

And once I realized that, and that light switch went on, I explained it to my daughter. And I also let her know that she's not short of any love, and the only thing she can do is pray for her dad, pray that something in his life and his heart turns around that will make him want to be a part of her life; but if not, she's not short on any love,

I believe that people should just live their life in gratitude and give. I'm a believer in giving and not holding on, because when you hold on to something you don't allow something else to come in.

And that hurt me. I've never felt hurt like that until I became a mother. I wasn't able to feel like I feel, now, before I became a mother.

One day, I was writing in my journal about him, trying to release some stuff. I didn't want to keep holding on to what I was feeling from him. As I wrote, I realized that he's never had a daddy. He's never even met his father. He's never seen his father. He's never talked to his father. So half of him is unknown. He knows who his mother is, but his other half is completely unknown.

To go through life not knowing the other part of your DNA has to play a part in your psyche. And to not be able to have an example of what a man is supposed to do once he becomes a father has to play a role in your

and to be thankful that she at least knows who he is and have something to identify with, because he doesn't have that.

It helps me not to hold anger. It helps me to look at people for who they are, and their life experiences. Once you can understand a person's story, you can give empathy and sympathy for what's going on and who they are, and not put them on this pedestal of where you think they should be and who they should be, but you have to authentically look at who they really are. Once you do that, you can't really hold a grudge.

I have definitely been hurt by people. I've been hurt by my mother. But once I understand who my mother is and what her lifestyle was like, I can't hold that hurt and that grudge towards her anymore. The only thing I can do now is understand her better and understand why she was not who I wanted her to be. You know, people do what they learn; they do what they see, and it kind of just trickles down. At some point, you have to say, "Hey, I'm going to stop this cycle here, and I want to do something different."

To me, God is love. God is not ego. And a lot of people live their life with ego. They don't know how to humble themselves and live their life through love.

Love, forgiveness, and gratitude are very important—very, very important —to live a fulfilled and happy life. And there's so much lack of love going on, there's so much lack of forgiveness going on, there's so much lack of gratitude, and a lot of ego that's going on, that I really try to live my life every day with love, because love is God. God is not judgmental.

I'm grateful for where I am. I'm grateful to be able to acknowledge God. I'm grateful for all the negativity that I have experienced that I was able to turn into positivity. I'm grateful to wake up every day and know that I am my creator of my life, because that's what we all are; we all are creators. We are made in the image of God, and God created everything, and He allowed us the freedom of choice to create our lives how we want. Everything you see was once a dream to somebody, a vision that they had, whether it's the bed, a chair, a dresser, your shoes. Someone had to have vision of it first. It was a fantasy. They turned into a reality, good or bad. We have the power to do that.

Your Infamous Mothers was once a vision, and now it's becoming a reality. Have fun with your creation. Don't limit yourself. That's it. Make the best of it.

From family to business, don't forget to live in the moment. Don't work so hard that your days pass you by and you have no memories. If you have to take an hour out of the day just to smell a rose and look around and just breathe in, do that, because you don't want to miss the moment, planning so much ahead in the future.

I've gotten to a place that was not easy, that's why it's my superpower: I allow people to live in their own truth. I can hear someone else's story and hear what their reality is without judging them. Everybody wants to be heard, you know, from children to senior citizens. Everyone wants to be acknowledged.

I grew up where I didn't have a voice as a child. You did as your mom said, and that was it. You didn't ask why or have a rebuttal. I was not heard. And when you're growing up not being heard, when you find moments when you can be all that you can be, it feels good because you're used to being shut down.

With my children, I allow them to have a voice, and I allow them to be heard. We have an open table. My daughter can talk to me about anything, and I'm so grateful to God that she does, regardless of how I might be feeling inside. And I check myself before I respond. But she comes to me about everything. And I appreciate that, and I hear her, and I acknowledge her. And I'm going to leave that there because I'm going to cry. ❖

Janet S.

I'm not a good mom. Ooh, Lord. I've hustled. I've been in the street. I was never home with my kids. My lifestyle was hustler, pimp, drug dealer, abuser, controller, all of that. People don't want to have nothing to do with me because of that, and when they look at me, that is all they see.

At the age of 4, I was molested by my mother's best friend's husband. I was brutally raped when I was 7-years-old. This incident would change the course of my life. The way I am today is based on those incidents that happened to me.

At about 8, I began stealing. At this age, I can recall trying to kill myself with a small piece of broken glass. I started hanging with the wrong crowd when I was 11-years-old, and by the time I was 12, I was an alcoholic and caught my first attempted murder charge. I remember my parents working with the mayor to get those charges off of me. I was fearless and didn't care about consequences. I did what I wanted to do.

It started when I put a knife to my dad's throat because of the pain he inflicted on me and my family. Hell, I was tired of him abusing us, abusing my mom in particular. She had to get her head shaved and stitched back together, and from that moment on I was extremely angry. I became abusive toward everybody. I became suicidal. I started cutting on myself.

As I got older, I started carrying myself as if the world owed me for all the things that happened to me—being molested, being raped, or being abused. No matter where I went, I had to fight. I fought at home; I fought at school; I fought in the street. I didn't trust anyone. If they cared about me, I didn't allow that in because I didn't believe them. It was hard for me to trust.

I became a mother when I was 18-years-old, with someone who was abusing me. I fought back, but I guess if he's still putting his hands on you, you're being abused.

And that quickly ended, that relationship. So now I'm homeless with a 4-month-old baby and nowhere to go. I don't have any family because they disowned me when I chose to leave home. When I finally did reach out to my family, they pushed me away.

I felt like dying. I think around eight is when I first tried. I was 8-years-old with a piece of glass, North Side of Chicago. I thought I was going to kill myself with a broken bottle off the ground. It was green. I remember. I didn't want to live.

I wanted them to see my pain. I wanted them to see that I hurt. I wanted them to see that I was part of the family, and I was their daughter, too. I wasn't being seen at all. I wanted to know that I was loved just like MV and Alfreda, who shared both parents together. We all had the same mother, but their dad was my stepfather. I felt like an outcast.

My parents are gone, and I don't have the chance to make it better. I can't tell them how much I'm hurting. I don't have a chance to be seen. My dad was on his death-bed, and he told the security people to take me out of the hospital.

I was 18 when I got pregnant with my first daughter, and I did that on purpose because I wanted something that could never be taken from me. I felt so battered. So here I am now 19, with a baby, with nobody and no support, no anything.

I started selling weed. Then I went to selling other stuff. And now I'm pregnant again. My oldest daughter is four months old, and I'm pregnant again with my second daughter—homeless with nowhere to go, sleeping behind bushes and having my daughter in respite so she can have some place to be.

Today, I'm a pretty good mom. I'm a damned good mother. And I'm even a better grandmother. I love my girls, and I refuse to let anyone come before my kids.

What's pushing me is that little boy. That little 17-month-old is running my house, tearing it up right now, just knocking stuff over everywhere, singing to me, trying to talk. That little boy right there, I love him so much.

I wish people would see me as who I am today and where I'm trying to go instead of who I was yesterday. I've got this catering business that I've been trying to get off the ground, and I would love my family to be a part of it. My sisters, I would like them to be part of it. I've always wanted to have a family-owned business.

I'm the third oldest person alive in my family, and I'm 42-years-old. That's a lot of weight, even when you're not close with your family, you know. My mom's gone. My dad's gone. Grandparents have all gone.

My office hours are from 8 to 4. My office is at home. Whether I get a phone call or not I sit there, other than running little errands like giving out business cards. I just got a sign for the yard. While I'm sitting there, I do homework. For the most part, I work as a private chef. The next phase of my progression is a food truck.

I'm in school. I need my bachelor's degree for this discipline, especially since I'm doing this on my own. And that's hard. I don't want to just be a dreamer. I'm not a street person anymore.

I have abandonment issues. When my daughter turned 18 last year, it got bad. I started feeling suicidal. She was 18 and still living at home. I wanted to kick her out, but then I remembered how I felt when I left home. I didn't want to do that with her.

I lost two kids to the system. My two older babies were gone by the time they were six or seven-years-old. Adopted. That put me in a psych ward. They took something that I thought could never be taken from me. Eventually, they managed to make their way back home.

I was able to keep Marie at home because I was married to her father. And they told him that he couldn't fight for the two older ones because he wasn't their biological father. He could only fight for his. So that's what he did.

I almost died being raped. It was a whole bloody crime scene. I started having out-of-body experiences, and they used that against me in court on my kids. I was homeless. And when I say homeless—with my kids, all three of my girls, I'm literally standing outside with this cup. I'm standing outside with my kids in May of 1998 not knowing what I'm going to do,

All of a sudden, we're in court and my kids have got a guardian ad litem. I can't visit my babies. I can't see them. I went downhill. I started pimping. I went around taping up "Now hiring" signs! I had the city threatening to arrest me if I didn't go around Madison and take down all the notices.

weren't going to come back home. My kids didn't come back home until they were grown.

I couldn't do group, but that's what they wanted me to do. "You have to go to parenting groups. You have to go to anger management groups." And I'm sitting in all these groups getting madder and madder and madder. I just stopped going. And then they used that against me. I couldn't win for losing.

Henry passed away September of 2009. And then my mom passed. That's what made me decide to get out of the street, after my momma passed away. That's all my momma wanted. My dad, too. Back then I didn't see it like that, so of course I cussed them out. But now that they've gone, I'm so sorry.

On the street, I stayed in jeans, gym shoes, toothbrush

I didn't know where to fit in in the world. I didn't know if I should love you or hate you, regardless to how you treated me. Anything good or bad that happened to me I was always angry, so I never saw anything good in it.

I had applications. There was criteria to the game. There was levels to it! It's funny now. It wasn't funny back then. I was dead serious back then.

I never dealt with this rape. One day I woke up, and I'm knocking refrigerators over; I'm tearing the house up. March 7th of 2000. My sister said I scared the hell out of her. She called the police because she couldn't calm me down.

They removed Glenna and Michelle from my house. I remember packing their clothes and making sure they had a picture of me and my husband, Henry, so they could take mementos with them. I felt in my heart they

on my ear or in my pocket. I'd move around town selling drugs. I'd be carrying my clock in my pocket wherever I go. I sold drugs all day. At night, that's when I did my pimping thing with my little top-dollar moneymaker. We was going to Fond du Lac, Milwaukee. I was taking her around the different clubs, even the strip club. "Let's go to amateur night and see what money can get pulled out."

I didn't know where to fit in in the world. I didn't know if I should love you or hate you, regardless to how you treated me. Anything good or bad that happened to me, I was always angry, so I never saw anything good in it.

I'm trying to be a very different woman. I want to be a part of society.

I don't want my girls doing what I did. I don't want them doing drugs, selling drugs, pimping, fighting, going to jail. I was in and out. I don't want my girls seeing that. I don't want them to be me.

Now I teach my kids that what you've gone through don't define you. I'm happy that I got something to share with my girls. But yeah, I was afraid to be a mom to them because I did not know how to teach them to be who they were going to be when I didn't know who I was.

I had a really bad breakdown May 11th and ended up in the UW psych ward. I was going to run my truck into a tree. I backed my truck up, and I was getting ready to run it into the tree. That was the first time that I felt like that in 11 years.

I was overwhelmed with the relationship that I was in. I shouldn't ever have gotten back with this person. There was just too much nitpicking between her and my oldest daughter and Jasmine and it was more of Jasmine she was kind of after.

I'm just going to give you a hypothetical. You and I, we're in a relationship, right? You've got your babies, I've got mine. First off, I don't give no damn if your kids like me or not, because I ain't here to date your kids, I'm here to date you. I'm going to respect them because them your kids. But I will not sit here with your kids. I ain't gonna smoke no weed with your kids. I don't need to play with kids at all. I don't play with my own damned kids, so I'm definitely not playing with nobody else's kids.

That's what she did with my kids. She was always hanging with the kids, being on their level.

I was starting to get overwhelmed with that because I loved her, but I wasn't going to put her above my kids. I didn't want to make my kids feel like they weren't loved.

And then I heard Marie was sleeping in her car at night for a whole week. She would get out of the house with my grandbaby and leave. She was taking Samuel over to his daddy's house, and she'd be driving around until she got tired, and then she'd park her car somewhere and go to sleep. And I was wanting to know what the hell... Why are you not coming home?

On May 10th, I called my primary care doctor and requested for her to call me back, because I wanted to voluntarily go into the hospital. I've learned my triggers over the years. I know if I'm about to hurt somebody or if I'm about to hurt myself. It took me a long time to learn that, but I know those.

The next day I went in and met with an emergency therapist who refused to let me leave the clinic unless I went directly to the UW psych ward. But, you know me. I'm going to leave anyway because I'm tired of sitting here waiting on whatever it is you're trying to do.

So I left. Later, I end up getting admitted. I went to the UW psych emergency rooms. I was so out of it that when they drew blood, there was so much blood and I didn't know why. I think it just started squirting when they took the needle out. I just started drawing "I hate my life" in my own blood. I stayed there for three days, with a safety plan to come home with my oldest daughter

If you've got mental health issues, the main thing that you should know is your triggers. For example, I have severe breakdowns in the month of April every year. That's the month that I was brutally raped. I'll start crying out of the blue. That used to be so depressing, when you're crying and you don't even know what you're crying. People, places, and things that you know are going to trigger certain parts of your mental health, you need to just stay away from.

Eleven years ago, I'm being hospitalized because I'm taking a seven-inch blade trying to stab somebody. I was stabbing doors. But I thought I was stabbing her. That's how I was in 2005. In 2016. Eleven years later, I'm able to call a doctor and say, "Dr. Bowman, help me."

I ain't gonna give up on my kids. That's one thing I'm not going to do. I'm not going to give up. I've got to.

I am somebody today. I am somebody.

I am a woman, a queen, a fighter, a victim. I'm a sister, a mother, a daughter, a hustler, a thug. I'm an asshole, a procrastinator at times. I'm a self-abuser. I am bipolar. I'm an example of mental health. I am a sample of anxiety. I am a loner.

I am a student, an employee, and I'm a grandmother. I am neither here nor there. I am an auntie, a daughter. I am a niece. I am a Chicagoan. I'm a Wisconsinite. I'm a giggler and a cry-baby. I am sensitive and I am a brick wall.

I have made mistakes. I have lied, cheated, stole.

I have fought. I have been rebellious. I have been bullheaded, and I have been an alcoholic, and I have been addicted to weed. I have been homeless and I've been high and I've been low. I have been in the middle. I have isolated myself from family and friends, but I have carried my faith and have at times questioned my faith.

I have been angry. I have been suicidal. I have been crazy.

I have been lost and even have been found. I've lost my way multiple times and I've given and been taken advantage of. I've been toxic and I've accepted toxic situations. I've learned and I've lost. I've won and I've battled. I've been to war and I've been robbed. I've been neglected and I've neglected.

I've loved and I've hated.

There's some who hate me, who want to see me fail. They want to break up those close to me. And there are those who hate the sight of me. There's others who want to see me dead and there's others who will never care.

Then there's me again, a ball of sometimes nothing but a ball of everything.

I am me, Janet. Yes, me. Hey, hi, and hello. I am not ashamed of me. I'm not afraid to admit I am not perfect. I'm not afraid to say yes, I have messed up in the past. I am not afraid to say that I have made mistakes. I am not afraid to stand tall and proud of the woman I have grown to become. I am not afraid to stand tall and say yes, I have my days, but with God's help we got those days.

I'm not afraid to stand here and say yes, I have not been the most perfect woman, mother, lover, daughter, auntie, grandchild, sister, friend, or even a self-examiner. I have not been a perfect person. My soul used to be dark and my heart used to carry hate. My mind wouldn't let me forget.

Yes, I am not perfect, but at least I can stand here today and say—no, not say—I can scream from the mountaintop that I am no longer many of these things.

I am a SURVIVOR.

I have survived what most couldn't even handle just in conversation. I can now walk tall and proud of who and what I am, but most of all I can stand tall and proud because I am no longer a victim. Not a victim of circumstance nor a victim of choice. I stand tall because you can't hurt me with your judgments anymore. You can't hurt me with my past because I already accepted who I am and God has already forgiven me before I even became a victim.

I stand tall because I am now a fucking SURVIVOR. Now you deal with my truth. ❖

Oroki

Let me begin by saying that I was groomed from childhood to be a "nice girl." I never embraced that title.

I've been a mother (unplanned) since I was 19-years-old. My three children, all daughters, are now grown up with eight daughters among them (no boys). It's taken a whirlwind lifestyle to appreciate motherhood. I appreciate my daughters' patience in putting up with my infamous past and my slips into being un-motherly then, un-grandmotherly today.

These days, I don't have children to get up. I don't have a job that requires me to punch a clock. I pretty much live as I please. Believe me, though, I paid my dues to be able to live this life I've created for myself. I LOVE it!

My childhood is littered with family secrets: childhood abuse, neglect, and undiagnosed mental illness, which led to an adult life of drug addiction, incarceration, divorce, lying, cheating, bad parenting, and outright infamy.

After 16 years of recovery from drugs, I found myself in a pattern of relapse. My oldest daughter and my only sister suggested I relocate from Chicago to Madison, Wisconsin, in 2004. I thought that sounded like a good idea, a chance to make a fresh start. That's not how it worked out. Within a week of my January arrival, I found myself using drugs in Madison. Me, who'd never had police contact, ended up incarcerated by August. I stayed drug-free for 14 months but ended back in jail after another relapse. Fortunately, I've totally surrendered this time.

Through lots of blood, sweat, and tears, I was finally diagnosed with bipolar disorder and celebrated 11 years clean last month!

I'm grateful to my mother, who allowed her two daughters (Rakina is my younger sister) to be free spirits, to think outside the box. We both chose African names to replace the European names we were given at birth. Our mother readily accepted this bold move and respected our choice. She also instilled in us the spirit of being community-oriented. We both have been part of organizations that demanded societal change since our early years.

In 1994, I founded an organization called Sisters on a Journey. We went on a brief hiatus during my drug relapse, but upon my return from Madison to Chicago in 2010, I reinvented Sisters on a Journey. Today we host a drumming circle, storytelling group, a writing circle, and vision board parties, retreats, and social gatherings. Our target is women survivors of trauma. Some of the activities are for the community at large.

Most of the women in our family seem to have inherited an entrepreneurial spirit. Recently I discovered the art of handmade jewelry. I have a full made-to-order jewelry line called The Obeah Woman Collection. I also make and sell baked goods. I was introduced to the adult drama ministry at Trinity United Church of Christ, where I've been a member since 2003. From there, I made a connection with the Hyde Park Community Players. Last year, I had a major role as Mama in *A Raisin in the*

Sun. I also directed a staged reading of Toni Morrison's, *The Bluest Eye*. There's now a fire inside that's leading me to start my own theater company!

I know that I am blessed to have the love and support of my daughters, Asabi Oluremi, Mandisa Izegbe, and Uchefuna Aisha. They suffered, were targeted and humiliated through the years of my drug addiction and untreated mental illness. Through it all, they've never stopped loving me. Sometimes I see them give-me the "side-eye"—even in full recovery I can be a handful. They know who their mother is. Asabi sometimes shakes her head and says, "My mother... Oh, here goes my mother again." Even the eight granddaughters: Asafoni, Nia, Faith-Kimani, Amaya, Akilah, Azaria, Layla (ages 22 to

felt. I've got gray hair that I'm coloring, but it's a choice, not doing anything to deny my age. Just yesterday I took my first line dance class so I can keep up, as I'm out on the dance floor as often as possible. By the grace of God and good genes, I don't have arthritis, I don't have high blood pressure, or diabetes. None of that stuff. I don't have to put on glasses to read. I'm doing pretty good. I get around pretty good.

It wasn't until the second incarceration in Madison that a therapist suggested I might have bipolar disorder. I'm: "Well, let me look into this." I looked at the symptoms and said, "Oh my God, that's me!" I know now I probably have lived with this since I was a teen. Owning out loud that I live with bipolar disorder allows somebody else to

It wasn't until the second incarceration in Madison that a therapist suggested I might have bipolar disorder. I'm: well, let me look into this. I looked at the symptoms and said, 'Oh my God, that's me!'

6) know that Groki (Grandmother Oroki) is not the ordinary kinda grandma. I'm cool with that and encourage them to get in touch with their own uniqueness, to embrace their own infamy.

My mother died in January of '99. She did all the holiday meals. She liked to be the person to cook all the food. The first years that she was gone, I felt like I had to do what she did. I'm the one who has the big house in Chicago. After a few times of trying it out, I realized I don't wanna do that, and I don't have to do it. Things are different in terms of tradition in the family now, and I'm okay with that. It doesn't have to be what it used to be. We can make new traditions. I believe my mother would be okay with my choice.

I will turn 64 in August, and I feel as good as I've ever

say, "Oh my God, I have the same thing" or "my daughter has that." I want to eradicate the shame that comes with having a mental illness, especially in the black community. My mission is to heal myself so that I can heal other the people who come into my world.

My bipolar disorder is currently in remission. I do the work to stay drug-free and mentally stable. I see a therapist once a week. I'm under the care of a psychiatrist and take medication. I'm also an active member of a 12-step recovery program.

I still buck normality and would rather have challenged the rules than lived a boring life of "playing nice." Do I have any regrets? Only that some innocent people got hurt while I was in hurricane mode. Yes, I am an infamous woman, a proud infamous mother! ✻

Janet M.

I was five months pregnant when I got married. It was a disgrace back then to have a child out of wedlock. It was not in my plans or life goals to have children at that period in my life, let alone to have sex with a man.

I wanted to be a nun and travel the world helping people and spreading the good news found in the gospel of Jesus Christ. My desire to be a nun arose up in me while in elementary school. I saw it as a means to escape my past of childhood molestation.

The males in my family and my neighborhood were so sexually driven that I had to run and fight and hide to keep their hands off my body. I was afraid of being raped by them. I remember a girl who was once a classmate who lived a block away from where I lived on the same street. She was train raped, and it messed her mind up. She and her family moved from the neighborhood shortly after the incident.

She was not the only person being raped during those times. There were many kids, women, and males being sexually violated. Some you knew of and some you didn't. So going into the convent at that time was my only reality of escaping the sexual dilemmas that surrounded me.

My first redemption was my shotgun marriage. Some might question how that type of marriage could be redeeming. I was redeemed from secretly practicing sexual immorality. I didn't know that the nuns and boys were being sexually violated during that time by the priests.

I didn't realize these atrocities were happening in the church until many, many years later. But today, a lot of young boys are filing suits against priests for what they did to them in their childhood.

The nuns that discouraged my entry into the convent knew I would not have been a good candidate. They knew I had good, loving, and caring parents who would help me through any kind of issues that I was having. What they didn't know was that my parents were not aware that I had issues. I was raised in an environment where children were seen but not heard. As long as your needs were being met and some of your wants, children had no complaints. Those children who did complain were considered self-centered, selfish, and ungrateful. And God forbid if you were curious. Ungodly curiosity got you into a heap of trouble. So those small, troublesome sins of mine were often discussed with the priest and nuns of my church community. They knew me well enough to know that I would not survive in the religious orders of the Catholic community, and they pushed me toward that of the secular.

By the time I graduated high school, I had feelings of abandonment from my religious community and ran to the arms of my husband, with whom I conceived three sons. We barely knew each other when we got married. We were strangers, cohabiting from our emotional feelings of abandonment. We often shared with each other our feelings of discontent, anger, and bitterness, and couldn't understand why a good and just God would allow us to struggle like that. And we vowed our allegiance to each other. We would conquer the world together independent of our surroundings.

By the time we had our second son, we were financially stable but had drifted deeper and deeper into the world of darkness. We had stopped going to church and pushed God out of the equation in our lives. As a result, we not only drifted deeper into darkness, the darkness created many conflicts in our relationship and caused us to neglect our two sons. By the time I was pregnant with our third son, we had separated.

that time. The issues began receding when I received the assistance and guidance of earth angels. That's what I call the people who surrounded me with the new relationships that I had within the Civil Rights organization—women who were deeply rooted in the belief and powers of Jesus Christ. They encouraged me to find and join a church that would teach me more about Jesus and His powers. I am forever grateful for their guidance. I found a church home which taught me to search the Bible for His truths and inspired me to return to my career goals.

By the time my youngest son was five-years-old, I had found an educational institution that accepted me

My experiences in Ottawa made me change my view of white people because it was the white people of Ottawa that opened the door for my change. The Ottawa community **treated me like family and taught me the meaning of forgiving.**

The separation had a brutal impact on our elder two sons. The conflicts I was having with my husband had merged with those of my youth and escalated my anger and bitterness, forging into hatred. My battle with my emotions became an affliction on my children. I had become impulsive and had no ability to stay focused. I didn't even know how to pray anymore. I was at rock bottom, and I needed to make a change in my life quickly, or I was going to end up in a mental institution or have a stroke.

One day I heard a calling from God to volunteer with the Civil Rights Movement, which led to my second redemption. It gave me an opportunity to shift my focus off my issues and focus on the issues of others. My activity with them redeemed me from the issues I was having at

and my sons in a small and rural town called Ottawa, Kansas. My family was not too thrilled about the change, and was not confident that I would succeed because I didn't have the finances to support me. I had enough grants and scholarships to finance my education. I didn't have the money for my housing expenses. But the university encouraged me to come anyway. So me and my sons left for Ottawa with only $250 in cash and much hope.

Not knowing where I was going to reside, without regret, I took that leap of faith. Nor did I know that Jesus had placed compassion for me with the university's administration and townspeople. They set me up for temporary housing in one of their dorms while one of their board members was completing renovation of a house, which he rented to me for four years. And the town's

female missionaries supplied my home with furniture and other accessories, which made my home comfortable for living. Now, my next concern was this: how was I going to pay for my rent and provide food for my family. They, the townspeople and the university, had figured it all out. I was encouraged to apply for ADC and food stamps.

Jesus was giving me a chance to redeem my past of anger, bitterness, and hatred. My experiences in Ottawa made me change my view of white people, because it was the white people of Ottawa that opened the door for my change. The Ottawa community treated me like family and taught me the meaning of forgiving.

I was also fortunate to develop a mother-daughter relationship with a black female minister who was highly respected in the community. She was another earth angel who kept me focused and anchored in doing the will of Yahweh. She was instrumental in teaching me how to practice the truths of the Bible and keep Jesus and the Holy Spirit close in all my decisions. She was a perfect mentor and example besides my mother and my mother-in-law, who contributed to me becoming an infamous mother.

I am who I am today because I had extraordinary women who helped me overcome my struggles with low self-esteem, shame of disappointing my parents, lack of confidence in myself, my impulse behavior, and lack of ability to stay focused, to name a few. Overcoming those things made me a stronger person. It made me be able to deal with situations, downtrodden situations, or issues that can impede your growth and development in the journey that you must go through in life.

I learned not to be quite as impulsive. I learned to have more confidence in myself. But first, before you can do those things, you have to identify the negative so that you can act in a positive way.

My abilities to be focused had a lot to do with my ADD, my attention deficit disorder, which means I was not organized in the things I did, causing my impulsive behavior to flourish. That contributed to my making unwise decisions and leading me into the negative feelings previously stated. I had problems of completion when things were too difficult or boring. I was easily distracted by new adventures, leaving old ones unresolved. I always thought I would get back to them later. But sometimes that wouldn't happen, which led to my feelings of being overwhelmed and disappointed with myself.

As a result of being able to identify my ADD and having strong people to help me with those behaviors, I can see if I hadn't gone through those things, I wouldn't be who I am today.

I can help those going through similar experiences see what faith and hope can do when you can endure your struggles and pain, which can be a temporary state of being when you learn from them and make the necessary changes that lead you in a positive direction to receive change and success.

I am tutoring a young lady in the Word, and she had a lot of the attitudes and behaviors that I have had. She's always telling me now how I have helped her understand a lot of things. I always come up with an experience or show her something in the Word that helps her make that change or adjustment in her way of thinking.

The superpower that I have acquired in my life's journey is the power of the Holy Spirit. He is my friend, my counselor, my advocate, and my protector. I make no decisions without discussing it with Him first. ✲

Lolita

Music helps me express my emotions.

When we were going through hard times, music was always the common thing for my family. It shows "Okay, we're happy, everything's all good now. Nothing to worry about."

Most of the time it was sad music. It was painful music. The music expressed that I was feeling a lot of pain. If my kids were listening to that music, they were understanding what I was going through. That's how they knew if I was in a good mood, or whatever I was thinking.

"Don't Hate on Me"—that song was a way for me to understand why my self-esteem was low. It was a way for me to quit hating on me. That song was a theme song for me.

I was misinformed a lot through my life. I was informed that my opinions didn't matter because I wasn't the oldest. That's bad information. That followed me throughout my whole childhood, adulthood, and I'm just now balancing that out within the last three years, when I graduated from college.

My son, he's the oldest. He'd always get to sit in the front seat of the car. And that wasn't fair. I did not know how to negotiate and bring about peace.

On Facebook, people tell me I'm beautiful. I tell them it's because I don't look like what I've been through. But it's my experiences that make me able to look this damned good.

I used to hate my life. I used to hate my family. I used to hate my background. I used to hate where I came from, and I used to say it out loud to people. Because I was mis-educated. I wasn't properly taught how to advocate for myself. I wasn't properly advocated for.

There's a lot of reasons I ended up the way I was. Going through college and not knowing how to advocate for myself (always being blamed for stupid dumbass shit), that was the hardest thing I ever had to accomplish. The hardest thing. When I tell you I was gonna quit, I was gonna quit. I was surrounded by people who weren't listening to what I was saying.

I don't know how to choose the right words sometimes—a lot of times—but I know what the hell I'm talking about.

That's how I became a waterhead, crying all day. It started when I was young. They picked on me all the time. I'm waiting on my mom and dad to advocate for me, but they never did. After I figured out why, that was even more painful.

When I started using, I gave up on ever finding somebody that was gonna help me. That was me saying, "Oh, okay, let me just help my damned self; maybe this'll help me."

Growing up, the music was always loud. Whenever there were family nights—Friday nights, family gatherings—there was drinking and loud music and loud talking. You've got to talk loud because you've got to talk over the music, and you've got to talk over the next person that's talking over the next person that's talking over the next person. We're kids sitting on the couch, we're trying to watch TV, but we can't hear it, so we've got to turn it up. That's how I became a loud-talking person. I never realized that until I got out in the real world—three years ago, four years ago—and they say, "Shhhh."

I was working inside a student life center downtown, and I should have known. It was a lot of talking behind my back. Somebody quit, and they wanted to make somebody else in charge of it—after I ran it for a year. They called a meeting, and then they were like, "This person is gonna be running downtown." I didn't get what they were saying. And then she said, "Lolita, you okay with that?" I'm like, "Yeah, why y'all asking me?" Because I spoke loud, and I always had an opinion, and because I did not know how to professionally advocate for myself, I was portrayed as confrontational. I talk loud; it sounds aggressive to people if you're not from where I'm from, or if you're not educated enough to understand what real confrontation looks like.

Because you looked at me as confrontational, a whole lot of doors weren't gonna open up for me. Nobody was gonna see my potential because you think I'm confrontational. So you're gonna make sure that I stay hidden behind that door.

When I was in school, this one lady, she helped me.

She got me the job in the school. She said, "You know how to code switch?" She said, "You're gonna need to bring your white girl." And I was like, "Okay, but I'm not good at that because to me, that's being phony." She said, "Well, sometimes you've got to do what you've got to do, Lolita." I said, "I'm not good at being phony, but I'll do what I can do."

I was a bad mom because I didn't have an education. I have a lot of street credibility, but I didn't have that degree. But I was smart as hell.

I couldn't teach my kids the basic skills of not to be so emotional. Any type of emotional conversation, they shut it down, all the way down. That means no communication. It's negative energy. It's negative words. It's: "I'm right, you're wrong. I don't want to hear that; I don't want to hear that; I don't want to hear that; nobody wants to hear that." They're not open to anything but their own feelings.

I took my daughter to orientation for college. I said, "You need to go to school. While you're gonna go to orientation, I'll go with you." We get there, and they show us the numbers. The graduation rate was 80 percent. And I said, "Girl, do you know what that means? They're helping their students graduate. I'm gonna sign up." I did. And she did. I said, "Maybe I can finally get the help that I've been hungry for, so I can stop the vicious cycle." I started going to school for human services, and that helped me change the whole perspective.

When you're going to school for human services,

you're learning about people and their attitudes. I figured in order for me to help people, I had to first help myself. Every project they gave us I made about me, so I could learn about me and why I was doing the stuff I was doing. Everything was an "aha" or an "oh, damn" moment for me.

That's some "white stuff," my kids told me. And I'm like damn! I'll stay in it so I can better show them, because that's what that's all about. Let me see you do it first. Let me see how this is gonna work for you. Let me see how long you're gonna stay in it and, most importantly, let me see how you benefit from it.

They do see a difference. Not the difference I want them to see. I want them to hold my hand—like literally—so I can show them exactly what it's gonna take.

I worked in human services for people who have disabilities. I felt like I had disabilities, so I already know where they were coming from. When I worked with women in the shelter, I made it my business to go there for them. Towards the end, I couldn't do it anymore because I felt like the people with seniority were taking away from my soul and that would have affected what I was gonna be able to give to the women. And so I quit.

I give them courage and inspiration and love—a lot of love. I know that's what they need because that's what I needed. They need somebody to listen. I would tell people, "I can't tell you what to do." And that helped them be a little bit more at ease. They want to feel like they be

long to something. That's where the love come in. There were some that had the wall up, and I would tear it down with love. I know how to do that because I lived in it.

My auntie always told me to go to school. She implanted it in my head. Mommy did, too, but she could never say the importance of it. It was always about the money, so that you could provide for yourself.

I've been going to college since 1984. Just graduated in 2013. I never had nobody to help me. Whenever I would hit a wall, I would just stop. I kept wanting more. I kept saying, "I deserve more, we deserve more, way more." You've got to want it. If you want to go to school, you can.

First it was, "Oh, you need a high school diploma." And then they started saying "you need an associate's degree." But before all that I had a felony. I said, "Well, let me get this degree because I know I'm smart enough to get one." I had to get it. It signifies me not giving up on myself. It signifies that I can walk alongside just about everybody. I don't have to be holding my head down because I don't think I'm good enough.

I could never be white. I can sound white. I could dress up like the white folks, but I could never be white—and I don't even want to be. I'm okay with being me today. When the struggle got so hard for me, I said, "Well, maybe I should have been born in a white family, you know," but all that came from no self-love.

At the Black Women's Leadership Conference, women gave me the approval to be who I am and be proud.

"You don't have to be ashamed, girl. Get over here and talk to me. As a matter of fact, take my number. You're gonna be alright. Girl, we're gonna help." Nobody was turning her nose up at you.

I cried because I was never, ever invited to that type of environment, not given the approval to stand tall and be who you are. There was so much power in that room, I can't even describe it. When I got home I was scared I was gonna use, because it was so much. I was tingling all day.

When I got to college, it was like, "What's your goals?" "Huh? Goals? What do you mean?" "Yeah, you've got goals and dreams. You know, we dream every day. Okay, well, write it down." "I don't know how to do that."

So then I did write them down. The teachers did not

well just fuck you up. I don't care if I've got to go to jail. I don't care."

Well, I've been in jail.

I wanted people to hear my pain. They couldn't meet me where I was at and see where I was coming from. Nobody wants to see you. Nobody wants to hear you because they don't understand. It's a whole lot of people that's lost. Their souls are lost. That's the way I felt, like I was being told that.

Music in my house gave us permission to believe. It gave us permission to dream. It is like reading that book about Cinderella and Beauty and the Beast. There was hope. Music expressed feelings. There was a lot of feelings going on in our house.

...people tell me I'm beautiful. I tell them it's because I don't look like what I've been through. But it's my experiences that make me able to look this damned good.

mind walking me through a process. That was an important piece. That taught me how to be able to do that for people, instead of going through life thinking that these people are supposed to know these things already.

I kept going back to school. I didn't know the importance of it. I just knew that there was money involved. I knew it was important to constantly learn something, whatever it was, even though I couldn't put it into my daily life.

I know people right now in my circle that tote a gun around because they don't know how to advocate for themselves. It looks like anger. It looks like frustration. It looks like, "I don't want to talk to you." It's a shutdown, a meltdown, a showdown. It's all that because, you know, "I don't know how to advocate for myself, so I might as

When I was young, I was thinking I'm just going to go have a baby so I don't have to be by myself. So now here I am raising four kids who physically can advocate for themselves—they go down any street—but mentally they can't do it. They're going to shed some tears trying to figure it all out.

You have to speak a certain way, you have to talk a certain tone, and you have to talk like you have education. And don't come with this Ebonics shit. They don't understand that.

Even to this day, I'm having a problem at work. I'm going to somebody, and they're just looking at my tone. They're not thinking about what I'm saying. They're not even giving it a second thought. They're just too busy looking at the presentation. "Oh, she didn't pronounce her words right. She might be speaking a little bit too loud."

I ain't never been no threat. You know, I'm feeling like I'm in a corner, and I need to get out. I've learned that if they ain't gonna listen, just shut up. Just don't say nothing. I don't waste my time talking to people that don't listen.

I do a lot of volunteering. I want people to see and to know that they've got to never stop fighting. Even though I gave up, and I quit, I want people to not do that. That was the biggest mistake I made.

I think about my kids growing up with me getting high and drinking and not properly knowing how to advocate for myself. One day I decided to not fight myself anymore, to get out and fight the world. Go out and just do it. I did it in school. When I graduated from college, that was huge for me. I didn't think I was going to make it. I made it through because I never gave up.

There's still some things that I haven't overcome yet, but I'm not going to stop. I'm not going to give up, and it's going to come. I don't have to be quiet no more. I can stand up for myself. I can stand up for you.

People are happy when I'm around. People got hope when I come around. That's what I'm bringing. I'm bringing love, sure! I am important! I am beautiful! I am smart!

I want to help as many people as I can, especially females. What I have experienced, I didn't have to. If somebody could have just shared their experience with me in a way I could understand... It's all about meeting people where they're at. The people that think they don't have what it takes to get to where they want to go in life, those are the people I want to sit next to.

I can sense when people are not confident about themselves. I can sense that you think you're better than me—but you're not. Yeah, I can sense that. That's my superpower. I can sense that you want me to come sit down and talk to you and give you a hug, you know, and just talk. I can sense all of that.

I want women to believe they can do better. It's all about what we tell ourselves. We've got to quit telling ourselves that we don't deserve better, because we do.

I don't know how we got to this point. How can we fix this?

You're going to pass it on down to your kids, and then you've got three generations of everybody fighting to express their anger and frustration. The daddy had the gun, then the son had the gun, then the other... So there's just generations of everybody with guns now.

What's the solution then? How are we going to fix this? Can we fix this? There's a whole bunch of stuff that we could be working on. Yes, we've got stuff to work on. ✽

Marjorie

I'm an Infamous Mother because I was raped. Not in the traditional sense—a sexual rape—but as in violating who I am.

When I was in seventh grade, on the last day of class, my teacher—a young white male, fresh out of college—called me up to the front of the room because it was my turn to receive my report card. He said, "You don't deserve to be promoted, but I'm gonna pass you anyway." I was a happy child, and academically, I didn't think I had a problem. He had just told me something I never knew. Throughout the whole year, he never expressed that I was in danger of failing. So he mentally raped me—academically. He violently stole my confidence. I was a talkative child, and I believe that he told me that I didn't deserve to move on because he was punishing me for being mouthy, opinionated, and disruptive. It felt spiteful. As a child, I didn't think of that then. But looking back, I believe that was an intentional act. He violated my academic capabilities. From that point on, it was always in the back of my mind that I wasn't going to get promoted. A kid in seventh grade, that's a vulnerable time.

I remember not having a good summer because I felt I wasn't smart. I felt I was below average. Once I went to eighth grade, I still had those doubts. I did my work, and I did well. Teachers didn't say anything to me, but throughout that school year, I felt something was missing—that I was not meeting the standards.

I became addicted. When he stole my academic con-fidence from me, I started being afraid, and then I started feeding that fear of accomplishing academic success. My fear became my secret addiction. My mind caused me to doubt who I was or what I could become.

Every year from seventh grade on, I felt I wasn't gonna graduate. When I went to high school, the same thing. My grades reflected that I was average and sometime above average. I was making Cs. I could do B work, and every now and then A work. I didn't think I was capable. In my mind, I wasn't good enough. I could not get there.

My senior year, a teacher wrote a poem, and she chose me of all the students in the class. She said, "I want you." She wrote this real nice poem, and she said, "I chose you to do this poem for me because I know you can pull it off." That's the first time I got a glimpse of hope—my senior year.

Prior to that, my principal stood up and told our senior class, "About three of ya'll are gonna make it, but the rest of ya'll are gonna be a bunch of riffraff." But my senior teacher, Miss Miles, she wanted me to do a speech at a college campus, at Grambling State University, and I would be competing against college students. She gave me a glimpse of hope.

I went on to college. I struggled, but I didn't give up. Then I went on academic probation, and I had to leave the school. I went back. I had to go to a junior college, but I passed my classes. People didn't scare me; my success scared me. I didn't articulate very well, so that's another thing I became addicted to. "You not good enough because you don't pronounce words like other people pronounce words." I began to get in my own way.

People see me as this person who's succeeding because I'm a postmaster. When you look at me, you don't see this person who don't have confidence. Yes, I have confidence in myself, but that fear stopped me from being where I should have been. I finally got my degree. I started in 1981, and I accomplished it in 2014. Currently, I am seeking my master's in counseling.

I'm thankful for the journey that I had.

What made me the woman I am today is believing what God said about me. I learned the difference between trusting what man says about me versus what God has ordained for me. Who I am today is because of my faith in Jesus Christ and how the Scripture says, in Jeremiah 29:11,

but He used those things for His plan. That shaped who I am today.

The first challenge God put into my life started when I was 19. I didn't know it was a challenge. I was in college, and my sister asked me to take care of her son. He was 6-years-old, and she was going back to Chicago. She asked me, will I mother her son while she goes back? That was the year I learned about stress. I was a full-time student trying to mother a 6-year-old, take him to school, take him to soccer practice. I was trying to have a social life and playing basketball for the university.

One day, oh my goodness! I was laying on the couch. I didn't stay in a dorm. I stayed in a house with my nephew. And I had all these papers to do, and I couldn't do it. I could not lift myself up off the couch because my shoulders were so heavy. I had to roll myself off the couch to

No man can define who you are. You might not matter to one individual— your next door neighbor, or a relative down the street or whoever— but that's just one person. I matter because there's someone that needs something I have, or some experience that I went through.

"For I know the plans I have for you," declares the Lord, "plans to prosper you and not to harm you, plans to give you hope and a future."

When you know God has a plan for you, even when everything looks bleak, you're thinking, "This doesn't make no sense, God, but I trust you." I am who I am today because I trust Him, and I trust His Word. That means I have to get closer to the Person who has this plan, who has this road map of where I'm going. The things that happened to me, He didn't call those things to happen,

stand up. That's the first time I ever experienced tremendous stress.

I ended up dropping a class at the last minute. When you put so much on your plate at a young age and it is too much for you but you continue to go on, you will get to a point where your body says, "I'm not going any more. Don't care what you do, I'm not gonna move you. You gonna stay here 'til you understand what's going on." That was the beginning of change in my life.

Years passed, and then the Lord started bringing in

more nieces and nephews for me to help raise by myself. It changed who I was. I thought my path was finding a man, a husband, having my own kids and raising my own kids. But God said, "No, I want you to mentor these kids, mother these kids who are your nieces and nephews." And I was obedient to that. I was obedient. It's not what I chose to do, but I felt that was what God wanted me to do. Where I'm at now in my life, I'm seeing why I had those experiences. I needed those experiences to get where I'm at now.

So many kids are being academically raped. Silently, they are experiencing what I experienced. I can see on their faces that something is going on. I don't want them to be detoured in life because of what someone imposes on them. I make a difference because my experiences of being raped and scared in the academic world allows me to empathize with children who struggle in some area of their lives. I am able to tell them their limitations do not define their future. Those limitations, in fact, can make them greater. I mothered my nieces and nephews when they came to my house. I was able to channel my fear. I was able to help them. I put time into making them realize they are special. They can do whatever they want. No man, no human being can define who they are. I had to make sure they knew who they were and not allow bullying or outside influence to affect who them. Society and people have a tendency to tell you who you are.

Also, I teach Sunday school. For 23 years, I've done this. When I'm at Sunday school and I see a child closed with who they are, I want to pull that out of them and let them feel free to be a child and not let the world come crashing down on them because of someone's belief of who they should be. When I was 10 or 12, I remember back then I said I would never be a schoolteacher, I would never work with kids. I just wanted to be a busi-

ness person, have a good job, maybe be a supervisor or a CEO. I wanted to be a manager, but I wouldn't want to be with kids. But because of the experience I had with the nieces and nephews and working with the children in Sunday school, I see the importance of what kids need. They need nurturing.

Now I want to go into helping foster kids, in the sense of going to foster homes and helping. I'm not the only child that had a need. I been working with kids in church for over 20 years, and I see the need. They need positive reinforcement. The time that a child is growing is not the time for negativity.

If I wouldn't have had my experience, I wouldn't know how great the need is for adults to show kids the alternative, working them through scenarios. If we help the children now, we wouldn't have as many adults out there learning about who they are at the age of 40 and 50. My job is to show them, before they get to 40, to have confidence in themselves. It's okay to struggle. It's okay to ask for help.

I didn't ask for help. I wish someone would've told me. A child needs to have an outlet if someone tells them something wrong. I want to make sure that kids don't go into a shell if they have some kind of learning disability. If they have some kind of slowness, whatever it is, that's not gonna define them. Working with my nieces and nephews and working with kids in church showed me that kids need us.

I'm important because God created me.

There is nothing, there is nothing that God created that was bad. When God created everything, He said it was good. It was good, it was good, it was good. I matter because I matter to God.

No man can define who you are. You might not matter to one individual—your next-door neighbor, or a relative down the street, or whoever—but that's just one person. I matter because there's someone that needs something I have, or some experience that I went through. I don't know what hole they're in. They could be in a hole of total hopelessness.

Let me tell you where I am now. I'm a postmaster. I supervise people. I got my degree. People depend on me. They come to me with their problems. I matter. I matter because my nieces and nephews are who they are be-

world gives up... but we cannot give up. That's why a person matters. If a person don't matter, that's the end.

My superpower is I have the Holy Spirit. The Holy Spirit breaks the fear chain, gives me freedom, liberty. I can walk into a room full of educated people because the Holy Spirit is in me. "You're just as important as anybody else. You just go in there. I created that person. I created you." I have HS on my chest—Holy Spirit.

Fear is the enemy. The enemy can use people who are

My fear became my secret addiction.
My mind caused me to doubt who I was or what I could become.

cause I'm here. If I wasn't here, God would have made another way. He would have found somebody else. But I matter for them. They look to me, "Aunt Margie, what do you do financially? What do you do spiritually? What do you do academically?"

I could tell them: financially, I struggle, but let me tell you where I'm at right now. I matter because my nieces and nephews are so bright, and when they come against a wall or something, I'm saying, "Let me tell you what happened with Aunt Margie in 1975 or '76 when I was in seventh grade. Let me tell you what happened to me. You would never know I went through that because of what you see now."

I tell them don't give up. If you give up, it's the end. If a family member gives up, that's the end of that family. If a nation give up, that's the end of that nation. If the

brutal and cause a snowball effect in a person's life. It just gets bigger and bigger. Until I knew that I was raped, until I knew that I was addicted, I could not change that. Until I got closer to the Lord, walked in the Lord and I saw myself, I couldn't see that that fear was from the enemy.

I went to Africa one year, and I asked the Lord to show me what He wanted me to see in these people. This was about 13 years ago. I said, "Let me see these people how You see these people." And He told me, "I see these people the same way I see you. I don't see them no different." That told me God sees me one way, and I could not look at who I am through somebody else's eyes. I gotta look at who I am through God's eyes. Once I began to see myself through God's eyes, I saw myself, a perfect being, perfect because God didn't make anything imperfect.

That's it. ✱

Jessica

I never understood the word passive. I was always put in the category of being a passive woman. The definition of passive, it seemed, was a person like me—a woman with seven children. But I always wanted to have kids, so I didn't understand the judgment.

People judged me, in their eyesight, naïve—like I was a stupid person. And I knew deep down that I wasn't stupid. That's what I had to build on. I'm not stupid, okay? People talked to me, and I wouldn't respond and use my words properly. If somebody asked me and I didn't know the definitions of a word, someone felt they were more intelligent. I felt if I spoke out, I was going to be corrected, and corrected to a point that I felt stupid, but I knew I wasn't. I always had to prove to myself that I was a better person.

My inside was on fire. I was a better person, a stronger person than you could imagine. But that was on the inside.

My birthright was pretty much taken away from me, if I can say it like that. My brother that passed before me, his name was Jesse. He passed, and they had me. When I came along, I thought I was gonna get all this love, but I didn't. I was skipped over. There were three other children behind me, but I was dangling. A child had died in front of me, and then here I come. I wasn't the best-looking child, so when I was younger, I lost a whole lot. I'm not needing someone to blame, can't blame my parents. But I kind of blame... I don't know who to blame, but the world looked at me as though I just didn't exist.

The finger was always pointing. "You don't look the same way. Oh, you don't dress the same way. Oh, you don't talk the same way." My self-esteem was less; it was torn, torn you know. But with time, I finally got confident. My self-esteem had to become strong because of the struggle that came with not being accepted. Today, I'm much better than my beginning. I am better than my middle. I am more secure right now.

I remember one time, at my aunt's house. I was a little girl, and she said, "Umm, she ain't gonna be nothing, but have a lot of babies." I don't know what she saw in me. I was 10 or 12-years-old, and I'm like, "Wow." All she thought of me was having a lot of babies, and I did. I knew I wanted to have a lot of babies, but for someone to say that's all they thought about me, having a lot of babies, that helped me to be insecure...

Men just always want to misuse and abuse me. I always would stand up and be strong about it because I knew that I didn't put myself in the position for the men to mistreat me. But when my hormones started kicking in, it was one of those things.

I think that I didn't know how to... wow, so much shame, so much shame. I feel ashamed about myself. Like now, I'm feeling very... My-my-my, it's like I'm not having confidence in where I'm going with this. I feel like I really don't have a story to tell. It's like, "Okay, what are you doing that nobody else is doing? You had children, okay. Your marriage didn't last. You had a..." I'm not strong in those areas.

I always, always wanted to be a leader. And then I was a leader. I always wanted to prove that I was a person that could stand up for her rights. Stand up and say I'm gonna support what is right, something as simple as the lunch fare going up. It was in seventh or eighth grade, but it was a cry for attention. Not only from my parents but my classmates and teachers, something that says, "Look at me." I didn't make the best grades, so I said, "You know what? Let me do something different. Let me strike out in a way that maybe they can hear." I said, "We're gonna do a sit-in. Form the circle. Don't nobody go to their class-room."

The lunch bell and the recess bell came. We sat there because our parents shouldn't have been paying all that dog-old money for lunch. Everybody, like 60 of us, we formed a circle, and I sat in the middle. Even though it wasn't a full circle because I got suspended and then no-body stood with me, I felt strong. But then I felt bad be-cause when it was time to be held accountable, no one supported me. They let me take the fall by myself. No one stood up and said, "It was all of us, not just her." I thought the others would say, "Jessica, I'm a go down with you." They didn't. I found out at an early age that if I stand up for something not to worry about it if others let me down. I have to be strong.

I've always been a person saying, "Together we stand, divided we fall," and people don't believe me, and that's where my confidence sometimes get torn. But that was then.

I've gotten so much better because of the torment, because of the people calling me "big lips." It was so sad, people calling me Larry, calling me... it beat me down physically, but my confidence over years and years and years and years and years, it helped me so much, it helped me so much because I never knew how to deal with frustration.

And then I remember my mom.

My mother had a 90th birthday party, and I was help-ing her out. My assignment was to do a whole lot of differ-ent things—the food and getting the house together—and it was just so much. I was so frustrated. I was crying, and my mother came. I was saying, "Ain't nobody helping me or nothing." And she said to me—she was 90-years-old—and she said, "You want me to give you a back massage?" And I'm like, "Back massage? Shit, I should be giving you a dog-old back massage."

I let my mother, 90-years-old, give me a back massage. And for some reason—and I stand on this—whenever I'm frustrated, whenever life beats me down so bad, I think about a 90-year-old woman giving me a back massage from head to toe, and how much strength it gave me to pull off what I had to pull off for that 90th birthday party with so much pride and so much confidence.

To this day, I get into a thought of that massage and say, "Okay, remember them kinks, get them kinks out, get them kinks out, get them kinks out. You can do it, you can do it, you can do it. You better do it. You better be nice. You better, you, you better, you better do it, you gotta do it, you better not be mean to nobody, you better help this particular person, you..."

It may be small to someone else, but it just gave me so much strength. I'm kinda babbling, but it gets me through a whole lot of frustration in my life.

The judgment comes in: "Who do you think you are?" And I'm not saying that I bring light on different things. But. Hmm judgment, judgment, judgment...

I'm with a group of people—girls, friends. To me, it appeared that they were using me, only because I wasn't speaking up. That was then. It was like, you walk in front of somebody, walk side by side with someone else, they were more noticed. Not that I didn't matter or anything like that.

Back then, my self-esteem was low because I was so intimidated by words. But I know how to stand up for myself more. I know how to speak up more. Even if the outcome isn't what I want it to be. Even if I have to turn the other cheek and get slapped, I'm still gonna stand.

Now, you can throw something at me, and it's like, okay, but at the end of the day, what do you want to do buy you a jump rope." And she said, "I got one." Every day, I would go over there, and I would take a few minutes at a time, and I showed her how to jump Double Dutch.

One day, her mom—she had a cast on her hand, and it was after school, and she was struggling, and she came with this bag—she said to me, "Are you Ms. Ledbetter?" And I said, "Yeah." She said, "My daughter told me she wanted me to bake you a cake." "Bake me a cake?" She

My inside was on fire. I was a better person, a stronger person than you could imagine. But that was on the inside.

about the situation? How can I still help you? How can you still help me?

I became strong in so many dog-old areas. It's like, then, people were judging me for being a coward. I'm not a coward anymore. I'm not passive anymore. I don't get flustered and frustrated when someone say that I cannot do it. I just don't take it lightly. Then, you'd tell me, "You can't do it, you're not gonna do it." Oh, okay, and I really thought I could. Now give me a reason why you saying I cannot do it. Because you say so? "Yeah, that's why." Why would you say that about me?

I was walking past the school one day. The little girls were all jumping rope, and there was one little girl, and every time I walked past, she was the only one standing on the wall. This was going on for a couple of weeks. And then one time, I saw something was the matter. The little girl hello'd me, and I asked her, "What's your name?" And she told me her name. I said, "Why do you never jump rope with the kids?" She said, "I can't jump rope." I said, "You can't jump rope?" She said, "No, I can't." She was in third, about fourth grade. I said, "Tell your momma to

said, "Yeah. All she'd talk about was you showed her how to jump rope."

That's what I want to do. That's what I do best. I do that. When I see someone being sad and needs some help, I'm gonna make sure they're okay. Even if it's something as small as one sheet of Kleenex. "Why are you crying?" "Because I need a Kleenex." "Why you need a Kleenex?" "Because everybody else in the class got a Kleenex." I'm gonna go to the store, and I'm gonna go get you a box of Kleenex. I just put it on the Lord's tab.

I was in my garden, in my garden all the time by myself. And these kids, the children, they were sitting, and they were watching me, and instead of me just letting them watch, I invited them in, and I gave them my time, and I said, "Do you want to help?" And they said, "Yes." And the mother told me, she said, "You know what, Ms. Ledbetter? My kid's been waiting, waiting, and waiting for you to ask them. And when you asked, they said they wanted you to show them how to do the garden so bad."

So, that's what I do.

So my purpose is—I'm just gonna spread the goodness

that I know. If I'm with someone who's got low self-esteem... like the lady I saw, she was on the bus, and she was sad, she was really sad. And all I said was, "It's gonna be okay." She looked up at me, and I said, "I don't know what your problem is, but I know it's gonna be okay."

I don't want to have fear, to not be able to reach out, because I had so much fear, fear, fear. I'm overpowered with fear, fear. Sometimes it's good for me because I take that step further; the fear pushes me.

I do that because I say treat people how you want to be treated. And caregiving is a part of who I am. When I look at a child, a person, a friend, a relative or just see someone I know, it's not about me; it's about them. I give a person what I want to be given. I give them time, happiness. I want them to have laughter.

People, they always say, "You know what, Aunt Jessica (or Mama or Jessica)? You've always got something funny to say." Well, that's because I want people to feel like I feel, happy inside.

When people can't do for themselves, I take care of them. I'm a caregiver. I'm pretending my feet hurt all the dog-old time, but I can walk. That means I need to take care of somebody, or help someone, from the heart.

Anybody can be a caregiver. Shoot! My grandkid's teddy bear is a caregiver. But you need to be the caregiver from the heart. It can be a cliché, you know—from the heart. But I mean seriously from the heart. When you take your time, all day. When you look at someone who can't see. They can't see. They may get on your dog-old nerves, you may not, can't, don't even like them. But they can't see! Oh, my God! They can't see! Why you gotta mistreat them? I always try to separate the personality from the disability. I do care. I do care.

I don't know what to say. It's just what I like doing. I actually enjoy sitting with someone that's disabled. They allow me to serve them, and when I serve them, they appreciate it.

I'm 60 now.

What really made me who I am was when my brother got shot. He was 11-years-old. He was in Tremé, Louisiana, and I was in Chicago. I got on my knees. I said, "Lord, I want to be strong, and my brother, I want him to be okay." I said, "Whatever negativity I had in me, whatever I did wrong in life, whatever come to me, oh God..., whatever come to me in life, if anybody is mean to me, please just let me be a strong and better person."

I grew up in a matter of a couple of hours. I can say that particular day made me so strong. That moment right there made me a better person to cope with life. I didn't even realize it!

My superpower is I don't give up.

I know how to make a bad situation into a good situation. I know how to make the best of a worse situation.

In front of the yard, we didn't have any grass at all, no grass. My mom, she used to look out the window and say, "We ain't got no grass! Why we don't have no grass? I love grass!" I made it my business to make sure the grass looked green, and it grew. It grew, and then I planted flowers. My mom never had flowers in her front yard, never, never until I moved down here. I had never planted flowers. But I knew: this is something I can do, because it's the right thing to do. You take dirt, plant, and just watch the beauty that comes out.

You know. Just watch.

Now I have confidence in beauty and nature. They work for me. Taking the worst of a situation and making it better. Make a raggedy porch look like somebody's spent thousands on it.

The ugly duckling turning into a swan, that's me. ❁

Tamara

When I go places in public, I always notice how people count my children for me.

"Wow, you've sure got your hands full." People think that's the thing to say to a mother of multiple children, but it really is offensive. When I tell people how many, they're shocked. They say, "You don't look like you have five kids." Really, what they're saying is "I had an imagine of what a mother of five kids would look like, and you don't fit that."

Depending on what kind of mood I'm in, I'll say, "Well, now you can reset what you think mothers of five children look like. Here I am. Nice to meet you."

I live in a community that some would say is homogeneous—mostly upper middle class Caucasian. And here I am with my dark-skinned self and my headwraps on, with my "afrocentricity," and people don't know how to receive me. They'll say things like, "You're so well spoken."

When I first became pregnant, I was working at a flower shop and a grocery store. I was like "Oh my God, I'm pregnant!" I had just gotten married. I was 20-years-old.

Because I was part-time or I didn't meet the 40-hour per week requirement, I enrolled in medical assistance. In Illinois, the way it works is, you're told that now you go to the county health place. I didn't have a lot of information. You know, what to do, where to go, how to navigate through the hierarchy of here is your provider, and here is your OB/GYN.

I had hyperemesis. It's like morning sickness that isn't just morning sickness, it's all the time. I was watching cable, and I saw this show called A Baby Story. I would see these mothers have these beautiful birth experiences.

But I was so disconnected from that because the county health care was so substandard. You feel like sardines because you're packed in a room where there's 100 people, and then the way that they talk to you when you come to get the services is like you're a number.

They tell you where your birth is going to happen, and then the provider you get is the provider you get. I wasn't comfortable with my provider being a male, but there weren't any other options. I didn't want to talk to him about my past, that I had sexual trauma. I didn't want talk to him about why I don't trust him.

So in the birthing process, when Jocelyn was being born, he gave me an episiotomy that I didn't need. An episiotomy is a laceration to the perineum—the area between the vaginal opening and the anus. He gave me a fourth degree one, which means from one to the other. So one hole connect to the other hole, one opening.

There was no informed consent. They didn't tell me what was going to happen, why they needed to do it. I was tearing, this is what was explained to me afterward. And so to facilitate the baby's head coming out, he cut me. He did it so fast, my mother was upset, my husband was upset, everybody was upset.

Jocelyn was born at 4:05 p.m. They had to give me sutures. The nurses were pushing on my stomach; I'm trying to start breast feeding; she went across the room; they.... All these things were happening that got into the way of what I thought was a beautiful, ideal birth.

I felt so disempowered and victimized, and I felt like a number, like a cattle that had like a tag on their ear with a number on it, you know. She doesn't have a name. She's number 52 in the herd. She's just here to consume services that we're going to give her how we see fit. She's not here to ask us for what she wants.

I remember my very first postpartum visit. He said, "What about birth control?" And I said, "No, no, thank you, I don't want any right now." He said, "You will get pregnant again." He said it like, like I was a, a breeder, like "If you don't get this birth control, you're gonna get pregnant again," like, "We need to stop that at all costs."

Now here I am: a married woman, an employed woman. My husband is employed. We live in the southwest suburbs of Chicago. Our apartment was almost $1,000 for a one-bedroom. But because I have this quote, unquote "insurance," I needed to be guarded when I tell people that I am happy about giving birth and building a family. I had to validate that to other people, because of my lack of income. And I thought, I should do something about that.

I started slowly but surely saying that this is what I want. This is where I would like to give birth. These are the people I want at my birth and having to stand up for myself eventually led to me seeking a midwife... and seeking alternative medicine and alternative care, more of what people consider a crunchy or granola kind of lifestyle, where everything is organic all of a sudden, and you're reading the labels, and you're like, "is this, umm, friendly for dolphins?" People didn't know how

to take that, because here you are, an African American woman, you're young, you've got all these kids trailing behind you, and you wanna tell me you're looking at this label, and you're challenging me on genetically modified ingredients? And I'm saying, "Yes, I am." "Yes, yes, I am. And I speak like this, and I dress like this, and I have five children, and that's who I am." And I'm not asking people to accept me anymore. I'm telling people, "This is who I am," and they need to adjust. This is what a mother of five looks like. This is what an articulate black woman sounds like, and this is how I dress.

When you see women who are proud to be pregnant, you hardly ever see someone who's got a tattoo on their neck. Do you see what I'm saying? I don't see me being represented. I don't have a tattoo on my neck, but I'm saying I don't see people who are shamed for giving birth being represented in a positive light.

It's really just a social construct of who should have the right to produce and add to our society, and these people over there, who don't have access to the income, who therefore don't have access to the education because they can't go to college, they can't afford it, right?

Are you being irresponsible for bringing a child in the world knowing that child is gonna be more likely to experience obstacles in life that are going to make that child more likely to commit crime and be a menace to society? Those are the words that we hear, and so there are women like me that are saying, "I am bright. I'm intelligent. I am loving. I'm going to pour all of that into my child."

As long as we are disempowered and giving birth at the same time, we're breeding generations of disempowered beings. And that's one of the reasons why I fight for what I do. And I say I'm gonna change the way people give birth. I'm gonna change the way people conceptualize being pregnant. I'm gonna make the woman with the tattoo on her neck and the 18-inch weave down her back believe she is beautiful, and that she deserves to have services provided to her that she designs around herself. It's gonna be mother-centered even though she isn't the upper middle class lady driving the expensive luxury car and living in a gated community. She deserves the same kind of experience.

I'm 33-years-old. My mother is about to be 60. Her mother, what her life was like! What her mother was like! When we have an expectation of this baseline of what normal is, that poverty is normal, then birth happens.

credit. We don't have all these luxuries in life. But we do buy. We spend money, and they capitalize on that.

I came from a dysfunctional family. I found myself in foster care at a very young age. I aged out of the foster care system, and then I found myself in a relationship with a young man who was very abusive. Very, very abusive. We had our great times, and I felt like those were really good, wonderful, loving times of times of laughter, you know. They, they covered up for the times when he was yelling at me, or calling me names, or hitting me.

Many of us start out from an area where we are disempowered.

I had to make a conscious decision to identify what I did want to be associated with, or how I did want to be described by people. It's very easy to be marginalized as a black woman, as a black mother, as a black student, as a black community member, as a resident.

Without guilt. Because that's our normal. Do you see what I'm saying?

If you look in the most famished areas of Africa, if you look in the third-world parts of South America, if you look at Indonesia, where natural disasters have wiped villages off the map, women are getting pregnant there. Sex happens. Especially when you're upset. Sex feels good, and we're afraid to admit that. Making love is wonderful.

It's a stress reliever, it's all these things. And when people are working a minimum wage job and it sucks, or they don't have enough money to pay the bills, what do they do? They drink. They smoke. They play the lottery. They need some kind of release. They make love. And the "powers that be" that control all of the wealth—that one percent—they know that. They're banking on it, because those people are also consumers. We don't have

Being sexually abused before I even reached puberty shaped who I was as an individual. I came into myself already a broken individual.

But I had this resistance. I had this inquisitive nature to ask questions. And I also had this fight-or-flight syndrome. And I was a runaway. I ran away. I had problems. I couldn't figure things out, and I said, "You know what, this is unsolvable," and I would run away from home. My home wasn't safe. The people that I trusted with my care, who were supposed to feed me, and send me off to school, they weren't providing the basic necessities that I was supposed to have. But the number one thing was safety; it wasn't safe there. And so having to run away and having to do all of those things put me in a place where I was then confronted with "Who am I? What kind of person do I want to be?"

And there just came a moment where I had to look

at myself in the mirror and force myself into certain realizations. I had to become like my own self-help author. Because I couldn't tell people what I had gone through.

I've been arrested when I was on a hospital bed. The doctor discharged me, and within five minutes I was arrested and taken to jail. With a dislocated jaw, a bruised rib, and a broken nose, and a black eye, and taken to jail. And I'm 128 pounds, soaking wet. This man is 220-something pounds. Do you think I attacked this man?

Being at the Sojourn House for me was like a safety net, but I knew I couldn't stay there long because it had all these women who had been beaten up for years. Women who had children by their abuser. Women who had not come back from it because of the drugs and the alcohol and all of the things that they put themselves through to cope. And they were looking at me like, "Look at you—you're young, you got your whole life ahead of you. You can go to college if you want. You can travel if you want. You can sing. You can paint pictures. Go do something." And I did. I ran away.

I left Springfield, went for a new job, went for a new life. I left everything behind. And that for me was a turning point. What I did for myself is I refused for those things to be enough for me because I didn't want to be associated with the statistic of being the African American woman who's been sexually molested or raped before the age of 18. I was. But I didn't want to walk around wearing that. Do you see what I'm saying?

I had to make a conscious decision to identify what I did want to be associated with, or how I did want to be described by people. It's very easy to be marginalized as a black woman, as a black mother, as a black student, as a black community member, as a resident. No matter what category you're in, you're still a black woman. You're wearing your skin. You're wearing your hair; your lips are thick; your nose is broad, your shoulders. I have to challenge the people who are looking at me and challenge the people who are refusing to give me services, or challenge the people who are writing articles in the newspaper about the neighborhood I live in, or what I look like or how I love, or what kind of job I work. I have to change the narrative. And the women who are in these situations, all it takes is for one little seed to tell her that her narrative is her choice.

I'm in the community. I'm empowering people. I'm educating people, I'm giving them information, and I'm supporting them through their struggles.

There's this agency that gets money. These people are being paid to be effective but are ineffective. They release reports that show disparities in health outcomes. That African Americans are more likely to have diseases. African Americans are more likely to be incarcerated. African Americans are more likely to drop out of school. African Americans have lower literacy rate. This achievement gap. They can report and report and report and report and report. We have all of these statistics and all of these facts. But when it comes to swinging a hammer, where are these folks?

I'm a lactation counselor, and I notice that having that title gets a certain amount of recognition in the medical field. Being a doula does not, however. Doulas are seen as these kind of hocus-pocus kind of folks that don't re-

ally get the same respect that lactation counselors do, because there's all of this science that backs up breastfeeding and lactation. So I can go through the front door of the hospital right. Being a doula, there's nothing medical happening here. So I have to kind of go to the back door.

But as a doula, I'm operating in an ancient kind of wisdom. If I stand next to a woman who's going through something big—you know, it's a big, significant part of her life— and I say kind words to her, (How simple is it to say kind words to someone?) she will have a better outcome than a woman who is in the room by herself going through the same thing. There are all these studies that will show that if I stand next to someone and I say, "You can do it, you're beautiful, you got this, keep going," she's gonna have a better outcome. I mean, do we really need science to back that up?

I operate in an ancient kind of wisdom that says birth is natural, that birth is something that the human body is already equipped to do. We have socially disempowered people in a way to where now there's a need for a doula to teach people to trust their own natural instincts.

I think my superpower might possibly be being able to connect with people on an emotional level, and being able to read emotions and to respond to those. I think that's something that people describe in me.

I can bring calm. ✽

Jessica O.

I was nervous to see the pictures.

Have you heard this saying: "I'm so glad I don't look like what I've been through?" Girl, if I looked like what I've been through, I'd be so ragged.

Even though I've been through so much within the past decade, I can still see beauty in life and in myself and in the world. I can engage in self-care going through all these things. And that's a new phenomenon. I've overcome so much. Whatever life throws at me now, I know nothing compares to what I've been through. It's a testimony.

Let me start from the beginning.

I was born and raised in a very Christian household. A lot of the choices I made, I made so as not to be an "infamous mother." Things that are expected of you: you finish school, you get married, you have children, you stay married no matter what, you pray for your man.

All of those things I did. And I realized that shit ain't for me. That's not what's working. That's not being true to who I am. What's being true is being powerful and not just accepting anything, and not just saying I am going to pray that he changes. That don't work.

I'm a mother of four kids. A black single mom. And as a black single mom, I have to work real hard, and I don't always have time to do all the things that I want to do for and with my kids.

When I first moved to Rockford, I moved there by myself, me and my kids. This was the first time I had experienced people assuming things about me because of my race, and I know that happens. But when you are in Chicago, you are insulated in the community where your identity is affirmed.

I moved to Rockford, and all the assumptions ("Oh, she's got four kids, she goes to that college"), and I am like, "I actually teach at that college!" But the assumption was always that I was struggling to make ends meet. It was a struggle—still is a struggle—to take care of four kids by myself.

If I choose to date someone while I am raising my four kids, I'd hear someone say to me, "You should raise your kids and maybe love will find you after they've grown." No, no. That's not real life.

I can be multifaceted. I can be a mom and a professor and still think I am cool and still have a dating life. I can own all those pieces of me. I can walk into a room with my bad shoes on. Oh, people say, you know, she's bad.

I think it's beneficial for girls to see their moms owning all sorts of different parts of themselves. They're seeing their mom do this and they are able to conceive of gender in a very different way.

I don't think it contributes to a decline of mothering at all. Because if we don't do mothering that way, we will have another generation of girls who will accept abuse, another generation of girls who will accept all sorts of things that they should not be accepting.

It's also very beneficial for boys that they grow up

seeing strong women.

American values have never been beneficial for women. Black folk have never fit that. I hear black men talking about women being at home, staying in the kitchen. That has never been the experience of black folks.

I enjoy cooking, so if am married, in a relationship, and I cook, I am doing so because that is something I enjoy and probably because I am the one suited to do that, not because of my gender. And that's the message that I want to teach my children, too. You do what is necessary for the household. You don't do what is ascribed to you by gender.

The take-home message from me, and I have to remind myself of this all the time: the stuff that you go through ain't going to kill you.

There have been times where I'd wanted to die.

Three days after my son was born, I got a call from the hospital that he had cystic fibrosis. My baby is three days old and the doctor is calling, telling me he's got cystic fibrosis at 5 p.m. on a Friday, and I have to sit with this the whole weekend.

I was at home by myself. My parents had come to Rockford and got the girls, and so the girls were in Chicago. I was by myself in pain, just me and this newborn baby. I tell his dad. His dad does not come to Rockford.

Four weeks later we were still going through the testing for cystic fibrosis, and my baby got thrush. The doctor says, "This thrush might be some infectious disease. It might be HIV. Thrush is one of the signs of HIV, so I think your son got HIV."

I tell you I wanted to die. I lay in my bed for a week because I had to schedule an appointment to go and see the people for him to go and take blood about HIV, and we still had to see about cystic fibrosis. Back and forth to the hospital. He must have gone to the hospital at least

twice a week from the time he was four weeks old to the time he was eight weeks old.

The only thing that I could do was lay in the bed and look up at the ceiling. I couldn't do anything and I had no help. Their dad came up there and tried to have sex. I told him no, and he did not come back.

I lay there and I thought:

"This is not going to kill me, as much as I want this moment to kill me. As much as I want to not make it through this, because I don't think I can make it through it, it's not going to kill me. So somehow, I have to figure out the way to keep going. I have to figure out the way to make sure my other children continue to eat. I have to figure out the way to make sure they continue to feel loved. I have to figure out to make sure that I'm still active. Because this thing ain't going to kill me."

That's the lesson that I've learned: that as hard as it gets, it's not going to kill you. So you better keep going. You have no choice. You can't lay there and die. That's one lesson. A fairly powerful one, huh?

Fortunately, my baby didn't have cystic fibrosis, and he didn't have HIV. He just had thrush for a really long time. He is completely healthy. But I think I needed to go through that.

I decided to divorce my husband in February 2014.

In my marriage, I'd experienced a lot of depression, a lot of abuse that made me see myself through his eyes. You stop seeing yourself through your own eyes. You only see yourself through the abuser's eyes.

I had started seeing someone else. A month after I filed for divorce, I spent a couple of days with the guy that I've been seeing, and when I went home I looked at myself in the mirror and I thought: "Who is this? How did I get like this? Like how did I get so big? When did I stop caring about what I looked like?"

March 15th, 2014. My baby was a couple of months old. I was like, "I'm going to work out every day." Actually, I didn't even say I'm going to work out every day. I said, "I'm going to work out ten days straight." I would work out for four days and then take a break, and my girls were like, "I thought you said you're going to work out ten days straight. You stopped at four, and you're going to start back at one." I would miss a day, and I'd have to start all over.

Working out every day was very therapeutic for me. That was my time, and my children knew this is the time that mommy works out, so we can either work out with her or we can just get out of her way and let her do her thing.

I really appreciated that. Even now they know this is mommy's time to work out. My baby would cry as I am working out, and I pause and give him a bottle, and I would jump back right into it. Now he's 2, and when I am working out, he works out with me

I want my girls to see that mommy invests in herself. I grew up seeing my own mom get her hair done once in a week without fail. She goes to salon every Saturday. Can't nobody stop her from getting her hair done. Can't nobody stop her from going shopping and buying what she wants. I think that is valuable.

I think the most important thing is making sure you set aside the time. There might be dishes in the sink, but this is the time that I have set aside for myself. If it means I lay in bed and read this book, well forget the dishes for that moment. You need to have that time to yourself.

The dishes are going to be there, and tomorrow there's going to be more dishes. And the next day, more dishes, and if you don't take the time to invest in yourself, you'll feel like it's overwhelming. The reality is, it is a never-ending job. You have to take the time to invest in

your own mental health.

I don't want my children to grow up thinking that they have to suffer in order to take care of themselves, or they have to suffer in order to love themselves, or to believe that there is something wrong with people who love themselves—which is something that black women experience all the time. "How dare you? How dare you feel good about yourself. You know that's vanity, and vanity is a sin." You know—not really.

We stay in these marriages or these relationships, and we think that it's our job to fix them. That's what black ship with religion. I identify as agnostic because I think that religion serves a function. One of its functions is morality, but some of the most immoral people are also identified as religious folks.

Do I love God? I love people. Once I was able to let go of all of the guilt and oppression in religion, I was able to love, and that's what God is. God is love. The Scripture says God is love.

That really had an impact on my parenting, too, because I don't believe that punishment is what's needed all the time. I think that love is needed all the time. There are

Black men have been socialized to not love black mothers. But hell, black mothers have been socialized to not love black mothers. We hate on each other. We hate on ourselves. We live in a society in which black womanhood is not celebrated.

women have been doing all along. We've been trained to fix people, to take care of other people's children, whether they are grown children or baby children.

But that's not healthy, and it does damage to us, and not just emotionally but physically. Black women are living with heart disease. Black women are having strokes and high blood pressure, and it's not just related to our diet. It's related to our relationships and our relationships with ourselves.

A lot of the choices that I made, I made based on things that were rooted in religion. Based on this idea that you have sex outside of marriage and then you get punished by pregnancy. And when you get pregnant, then you marry the person that you are pregnant by and then you just suffer through it.

I've had some real come-to-Jesus meetings with myself about how do I feel about religion and my relation-

moments that my children will do things that ain't right. And I know there are folks who'll say you just got to beat them. And I am like, "No, you just got to love them. You have to talk to them. You have to explain to them the way the world works. You have to explain to them that not everyone sees things the way that you see things. You have to love them." I think it really boils down to love.

Years ago, when I first got married, I thought, at least he'd married me. Now I wish he hadn't. I don't have any regrets. I loved him and still do. But my marriage was devastating to me. Financially devastating. Emotionally devastating. I became his version of me.

I had two cars that were in my name. I had a house in my name. Then we got married, and all those things became ours. He took my first car. Sold it. We had this other car. He took that car and traded it in for something I could not afford to pay for by myself.

I go on bed rest with my first daughter, lost my job. He pays the mortgage. He pays the car note. When he decides to leave me, I lose my house. The car gets repossessed. I moved in with my parents—three kids, and one bedroom in my parents' house.

One of the problems we have is that we don't tell our stories. We are ashamed of our stories. These experiences continue to happen to women and we are so interconnected, but we just don't know it. Some of us are even interconnected with the same dude, and we don't even know it.

Black men have been socialized to not love black mothers. But hell, black mothers have been socialized to not love black mothers. We hate on each other. We hate on ourselves. We live in a society in which black womanhood is not celebrated.

Black women tend to be more educated than their eligible partners, which then makes them less eligible. Black women end up remaining single for longer. We are getting married later, and in getting married later, our marriages are more successful. Age is the number one indicator of divorce. The earlier you get married, the more likely you are to get divorced. The later you get married, the more likely your marriage will be stable and intact.

It is important for my kids to see me hurt. It is important for my kids to see me jubilantly happy. It is important for me that my kids see me work. If our kids see all the different parts of us, then they can identify with all the different parts of us.

I exist for me first. First because if I don't take care of myself, then I can't take care of them. In fact, me going to work is taking care of them. Me being healthy and whole is taking care of them. ✤

Sagashus

I remember vividly the times I've had to dig my car out of the snow—pregnant, my children and I using buckets because it hadn't yet dawned on me that maybe I needed to buy a shovel. I guess to do so would be to admit that I was away from all the men in my family, or that I was really, truly a single mom.

Shovels, like power drills and screwdrivers, are men's things. And since I am not a man, it never occurred to me that I would need them. And it never occurred to me that my parking stall wouldn't just magically clear itself because I am a woman. So I remember all the times I was late leaving or coming because of my stubborn refusal to accept that I had no one, no man, to do this work for me.

✻

It's summer, or maybe spring. Either way, the year is 2006 and the weather is beautiful. I round the corner and see my dad sudsing his maroon, four-door, short-body Cadillac. He sees me and lights up. "Hey, girl. What's wrong witcha?" he asks, still smiling.

I shrug. "Nothing." I say this because even though I am unhappy, it's my default mood. There is no beginning or end, a general sense of constant vulnerability. It's my normal.

"Aw, girl, I know it's something. Whenever that head of yours hang to the side like that, it's something. Look here girl. You just got your degree. You suppose to be happy. Look at all you've done."

It took me seven years and three babies to complete a four-year degree. It hadn't been long after I crossed the stage that he and I had this encounter—some days, maybe weeks, after. Moving in that uneasy way he and my sister both moved in, nervously shifting their weight from side to side and always smiling, he said calmly, "I know what it is. You can't see your accomplishments past all of your failed relationships."

Something quickened in me. He had spoken right through me, to what felt like my cells and DNA, to a loneliness and despair so inherent it felt genetic, and in return, at the core of my being, something understood.

✻

I am surrounded by women like me—accomplished, beautiful women whose lives are the sum of their relationships. Once, I was talking to an elder in the family. "She's a doormat," she said about another woman. "And you should understand that, because you were once a doormat, too."

Impulsively, I responded, "Well, if I was a doormat, I got it honestly. My brother, when he was a little boy, he used to watch you beg your man to not leave. He watched you on your hands and knees, crying, screaming for him to stay. More than a decade later, I watched the same thing. As the years went by, I watched you move from begging on your knees to begging on your feet. But either way, he'd leave. That taught me early on, if a man is going to leave, he's going to leave. But he's going to leave me standing."

This woman was one of the first in her family to go to college, to complete her degree, and to do something respectable. Yet, despite her accomplishments, there she was, on her hands and knees, begging as if her life depended on it, desperate as if his staying would make all the difference. Not her accomplishments but his presence would determine the quality of her life.

I am talking to another woman. And she is telling me about the days her mother would leave her in the car for hours as a little girl, how she'd disappear into various homes of different men leaving her to play alone with stuffed animals. I wonder now about the conversations she must've had with what I imagine to be yellow or green unicorns or brown, fluffy bears with big eyes. I wonder how she felt when her mother would say, "You stay here, now." Or how she felt when she would emerge what I imagine to be well after the street lights came on. How was the ride home?

Her mother—a very successful woman with big beautiful legs and round eyes, a homeowner, the owner of a beautiful, luxurious car, a hard worker, an entrepreneur—never managed to sit in the moment, to enjoy the now. Like me, she could not see her own accomplishments beyond all of her failed relationships. As I grew from sitting between her legs getting my hair braided to sitting at her table with a child in my own belly, appreciating good food and good music, jazz, I listened to a conversation that never changed. "Men are suppose to protect women,

to love us! We're not suppose to work this hard. I'm not suppose to work this hard, but I have to, because I don't have a man."

As a child, I watched an elder woman affectionately loop her arm around the arm of a man who married into her family. She was fond of him. When his children spoke of him, others would light up and join in. When I'd speak about my dad, the house would turn cold, silent. People would become suddenly busy, talk under their breath dismissively, no one making eye contact with me. I learned early on that a girl's sense of self-worth is tied to people's opinions of her father. I also learned quickly that as long as a man provides well and has a strong sense of culture, other things can be tolerated—like blackening a woman's eye, beating her or locking the children out on the back porch to sleep all night with the cats. I learned how easy it was to turn one's head to the mistreatment of women and children, how easy it is for women and children to turn our heads to our own mistreatment, as long as he comes home with good food and good music.

By the time I became a woman, my own accomplishments did not matter much to me. They always seemed to be tainted by the fact that I had no one to share them with. That stain was about something more than the usual loneliness associated with not having a companion. Rather, it was about a strong sense of inadequacy and failure. It was about a belief that was so widely accepted by me that it felt like an inescapable fact. I was *less than* because no one had chosen to commit to me.

＊

I remember the day of high school graduation being dressed in the all-white every female graduate was required to wear. In a long flowing white dress whose front overlapped forming a V-shape at my chest, I appeared regal, poised. I wore white, wedged, open-toe heels. Some might even consider my long neck and legs sure signs of gracefulness—had I not been stooped down banging on the basement window of the guy I was involved with. It was one of the most important days of my life, and there I was, trying to pull him from his bed to convince him to go with me, watch me graduate, support me. So much depended on his being in the bleachers, cheering. I banged furiously, desperately.

He knew we were coming to get him. He knew what day it was. Why was he doing this? Four years I had worked—staying up all night most nights my freshman year, trying to adjust to the learning curve that happens when going from an entire elementary school career at a Catholic institution on Chicago's Southside to the

rink, amazing food, an unrivaled education. It was good, hobnobbing with the haves. And when I wasn't having the ball of my life, I was arguing with the love of my life, surviving the multiple breakups, dealing with his expulsion, struggling with the challenges of puberty like heavy menstrual cramps, migraines, long hours in the infirmary, and severe senioritis.

Yet, there I was on graduation day beating on the window of a guy who never even bothered to move from his bed and face me and my disappointment. I imagined him just rolling over and pulling closely whatever woman he might've been laying with, and drifting comfortably back into his dreams. Needless to say, I showed up, late, without him. And found a way to graduate without him.

＊

This seems to be a consistent trend in my life. The whole reason I went to that boarding school in the first place is because I was heartbroken. The guy I really liked

I am no damsel in distress, and I don't need saving. And yet, I want to be saved because as fairytales have it, every damsel in distress gets her escape from a life of drudgery, and she gets her prince, her happily ever after.

beginning of a high school career at a private boarding school located in the northern suburbs, probably one of the wealthiest places in this country. Old money. I was proud of myself for being better adjusted by sophomore year, for having cuffed one of the most popular and talented boys in the school, and just for landing myself in an environment like that: beautiful trees, a pond, an ice

in grammar school just didn't like me. He preferred someone a lot lighter, a lot shorter, a lot cuter. That also seemed to be a trend in my life—being with guys who thought I was "perfect," but as one put it, "wished I was packaged differently." Someone I know suggested I was easy to shelve. "You are like a Pepsi bottle. Someone can open it, sip from it, put the top back on, and put it away.

But a can, well, when you open it, you have to commit to drinking the whole thing." And in retrospect, that's probably some of the dumbest shit I ever heard. First of all, it's just not true. I grew up watching an aunt of mine stuffing tissue into the opening of soda cans so that she can save them for later. People find a way to preserve, to enjoy, to commit to what they want. But beyond that, it's dumb because I fell for it. I let some guy and his talk about soda containers define me, like I had let so many others who had come before and after him do the same.

❄

I'm too tall, my hips too wide, breasts too full. Beyond these, my skin's too dark, hair too short, cheekbones too thick, too high. My education overqualifies me. I know too much, expect too much. As one guy put it when I was younger, I was "built for hard labor." I come from a long line of Harriet Tubmans and Harriet Jacobs, Anna Julia Coopers, Janie Crawfords, Aminata Diallos, and Onyesonwus... women in fact and fiction who are strong... heroines and crusaders. Powerful women, giants, African and African-American Amazons, tough, warrior females. I am no damsel in distress, and I don't need saving. Yet, I want to be saved because as fairytales have it, every damsel in distress gets her escape from a life of drudgery, and she gets her prince, her happily ever after.

II.

I'm a little girl, no more than five, maybe six... but I'm thinking much younger. I'm lying on my back, staring at the woman who is to become my father's wife. She sits on the stairs holding her two boys. Or was it just one? They're all (or both) watching, looking down at me. I'm looking back at them as this grown man puts his face in my private parts and licks me in a place that tickles. Something about this is wrong. I know it is. Even though he openly teaches me how to blow circles with cigarette smoke, and he sniffs lines of cocaine in our living room with me sitting at his side, I know something is not right. But I'm having fun. Someone is paying attention to me, taking an interest in me, laughing with me. I feel special. My mom says I shouldn't go in the basement because there is a guy who lives there, our tenant. But I sneak there anyway because even though I have my instructions, how bad could it be? How dangerous could he be? He's nice. And he lives in my house. So he must be safe and good, right? Besides, this woman my dad is to marry, she's there—walking back and forth, back and forth, saying nothing, as I run through the house, indifferent, as if I am a much older child who is bent on doing things my way, who has to learn the hard way, or as if he and I are a couple, and she is merely turning her head to our indiscretions. I am not sidled up next to him, that's not the appropriate word. No... no... no. What do you call it when someone sits awkwardly next to someone? When the other person is tall and sure, and you, that someone, are swallowed in the separation of two couch pillows, uncomfortably sitting next to the other, as if riding on a horse, but not able to sit in the saddle, and so you are flung about on either or all sides... awkward. I guess that is the only word to describe it, not clumsy or weird but awkward. Night after night, I sat awkwardly by a man who was licking my little girl parts and teaching me how to blow neat circles with the smoke from cigarettes and marijuana and how to snort cocaine while my stepmother sometimes watched, sometimes turned her head, but all the time said nothing. And there I was pressed up against this man, as if we were cuddling, except his arm was not around me. And I was swallowed by pillows way too big for me. Everything was too big for me. Yet, this was the league I was in, and as wrong as it was, somehow it was my life.

✽

"How can you guard and protect something that was taken from you so early?" I remember saying this to someone about my innocence. How can you defend something that seems no longer defendable? My head is toward the sky. I'm taking a deep breath, thinking. It's been over a year since it became clear to me that I have boundary issues. I was 35 years old and pregnant with my sixth child by yet another man who was somehow linked to another woman. I'm desperate. This should not be happening again. I've grown beyond this. I'm better than this. I'm cured. Yet, here I am back making the same decisions again. And I'm not going to make it through this pregnancy either sane or alive unless I get to the bottom of this.

"Girl, you're like a Cracker Jack box, every time someone goes in, they get a prize." My grandma would say this every time I showed up pregnant again.

My mother often says that I have no vices. I don't drink. I don't smoke. "All she likes is her sex. That's her only vice."

"You're fast."

"Just hot in the ass."

"Six kids. Damn... It. Must. Be. Good."

✽

For women and men on my dad's side of the family, sex was about business as much as it was about pleasure. But for me, it was always about something different.

Bartering. Sex has always been about that for me. I give you my vagina, and all that's inside it, if you give me companionship. It's all I had. I had nothing else of value. I had no money, for example. In our economy, in the open market of my community, my intellect was not valuable. In fact, the smarter I was, the more my worth depreciated. I've always believed I was attractive. But I accepted that my brand of beauty had no value here and that maybe it did someplace else. Like a Canadian coin or a British pound, my beauty had worth in another system. I just didn't know what system or where. What I did know was that I needed to be validated. I needed a man to affirm me, to hold me, to make me matter. And the price for that validation was sex. So I gave it up.

It was wrong to say that I was like a Cracker Jack box. I was more like one of those machines with the claw. You know, the ones you stick your money in hoping you get one thing, yet, no matter how hard you strategize, you always got something else? I was that thing. I wanted love and validation, but I kept getting babies instead. I was too scared to demand protection, afraid I'd scare off this him or that him. Too scared to wear protection.

III.

In graduate school, I read a piece called "Faking Motherhood." According to it, women fake motherhood like we fake orgasms. While I cannot recall the author's name, I won't forget her article. It gave me language for my own early mothering experiences.

It's true. I was faking it. In the same way I had watched enough television to know how to perform sex—how I should sound, how I should look, how I should act, how I should end—I had watched enough television to act out motherhood. I knew what "good" mothers said and did. I knew how they dressed and behaved, how their children behaved. If television wasn't enough, I had magazines. And if they weren't enough, I had the teachers and PTO moms, school nurses, family doctors, and churches. There was always some reminder—some form of surveillance, some kind of assessment, some variety of judgment—always there to show me (and you) how motherhood should be done. And so I did it, for years, just as I had been taught (and pressured) to do it. I put my children in the best schools. I fed them the best foods. I made sure they listened to bedtime stories and watched no television. I sacrificed and changed my life. I mothered well... and I hated it.

Caring for my children had become a very ascetic thing. It was all about self-denial for the betterment of them. It felt like one of those strange dystopian or sci-fi

maternal voice and identity. In doing so, I realized that it was not motherhood I hated. It was the conditions under which I mothered that I abhorred—the poverty, the judgment, the isolation. It was the mommy wars and the mythologizing that made caring for my own children difficult. More than these, it was my own sense of inadequacy and brokenness that made the fulfillment of motherhood feel unrealistic. I didn't value myself. How could I value smaller versions of me if I struggled to find the original worthy? In order for me to stop faking, my mothering practice had to become about me as much as it had to be about my children. I had to fully address me as I addressed them, if we were going to make it through this whole and healthy.

Bartering. Sex has always been about that for me. I give you my vagina, and all that's inside it, if you give me companionship.

movies where one group forces another one into concentration camps (more real than fake) or humans become slaves to aliens. It choked and grabbed me. I had become a rat in somebody's cage or some kind of subject in somebody's experiment. I had no free will. I was simply an extension of other people's expectations, walking on a tightrope... failure was inevitable.

Reading that article changed everything. It gave me permission to be honest. I was faking. I could say out loud, while alone (of course), "I hate being a mother." That admission not only unburdened me, but it opened the floodgates to new realities. It was the beginning of me trying on my truths. It was the start of me testing my

IV.

The summer I moved to Madison, I read two quotes that set the tone for my new journey. The first came from Rick Warren's *The Purpose Driven Life*. "Your birth was no mistake or mishap, and your life is no fluke... Your parents may not have planned you, but God did." The second came from Marianne Williamson: "Our deepest fear is not that we are inadequate. Our deepest fear is that we are powerful beyond measure. It is our light, not our darkness that most frightens us. We ask ourselves, 'Who am I to be brilliant, gorgeous, talented, fabulous? Actually, who are you not to be?'"

My parents did plan and want me. That was not my

problem. Instead, I was unsure about whether or not this new place could accept and make room for my reality. I had multiple children by multiple men. I was smart but had poor study habits. There was addiction and alcoholism in my family. I had cousins that I housed and took care of. They were as much of a priority as my children. So much of my life was inconsistent with the academy's expectations of what it meant to be a serious student. I had survivor's guilt, and I was fiercely loyal to home and my community. Could this place handle that? The Warren quote helped me manage some of my fears because it reminded me that I was no accident. I had a right to be here, regardless of my history and circumstances. This af-

We were powerful beyond measure, beautiful, boundless beings with unbridled capabilities. But for some reason, we stay so contained, hushed. Whether it was because we were our own best-kept secrets, hiding ourselves from the world, or it was because we didn't know our own truth, we played small and required each other to do the same. We shackled ourselves with vices— drugs, alcohol, unhealthy relationships—to cope, to forget, to keep our power in check. But this Williamson quote made me remember. It made me vaguely recall something that I once knew in childhood: I was made to be great. I just needed to remember what that meant.

I'm desperate. This should not be happening again. I've grown beyond this. I'm better than this. I'm cured. Yet, here I am back making the same decisions again.

firmation was something I had to come back to time and time again, as it was clear to me that I was, indeed, a different kind of student.

The Williamson quote made me think that maybe my anxiety was not about failing. Maybe I was afraid to release my power. So much of my life had been about playing myself small so that I could be manageable, palm-sized. I turned down my shine and made myself palatable so that I could fit in. I was always amputating bits and pieces of myself to make other people comfortable. In my heart, I was a goddess, as tall and wide as an oak tree. I saw all my friends, family, and lovers in the same way. We were all larger than life, giants walking the earth.

*

I used to bake cookies and sell them at recess. When I was a little girl, I used to design and make my own clothes. Every week, I dialed zero to speak to the operator and asked her to connect me with White House. I believed I could speak to the most powerful person in this country—and maybe the world.

As a grown woman, I realized that if I were going to excel, I had to reconnect with the little girl I was— an entrepreneur, a creator... someone who was confident. The more life I lived, the more distant she and I became.

One of my first memories of us working our way back

to each other comes from the work I was doing on metaphors. As an English major, I knew that a metaphor was a figure of speech. I knew that it was calling something that wasn't as if it were. But when I started studying the theory of metaphors, I learned more. I learned that in connecting these two disconnected things something altogether new was created. And I began to wonder if I were like a metaphor. I was a single mother with a bunch of kids from a bunch of dads. I was from an impoverished background, and yet, I was a graduate student. I represented the coming together of two unlikely worlds. Was I the embodiment of something new? Was I the voice of unexplored issues? Could I expose hidden challenges? Would being this new thing allow me to discover unchartered territory in feminism and African American studies? Would it allow me to talk about old things in new ways? I wondered.

Around this time, I had become a fellow with a research and ethics program on campus. My stint there also made me think. At the center of my work were the extraordinary of marginalized black mothers. Yet, they were not (nor would they be) the direct benefactors of my research. They were not my students. In the seven or eight years I taught at the University, I had less than three black or brown moms in my classes. In fact, I rarely taught people of color at all. My classes, like most classes on campus, were filled with young, white faces. Was it ethical, then, for me to build a life from research about a population that would never benefit from it? On a different but similar note, my own son was struggling in school. I saw him being pipelined into the prison industrial complex. Was it ethical for me to give some of the most privileged students in this region the best of my instruction when my own child was floundering and flailing about? I had to make a decision.

For one of our ongoing education sessions, I learned that the job climate for literature majors was pretty dry. Folks were not hiring us. And while some argued that my fate would be different, the uncertainty of whether or not I'd receive a tenure-track position gave me the encouragement I needed to venture off and try something new. For the first time since I was a child, I listened to the little girl in me and decided to seriously pursue my interest in entrepreneurship. My research was going to be the heart of my business.

❊

What if I could use everything I had gone through—the childhood molestation, the years of insecurity, the multiple children by multiple fathers, the addiction and alcoholism in my family... my interest in business... my beautiful education—for an occasion like this? I had two ethical problems to address. I also had to earn a living. What if my experience and my education gave me to the tools to create something unheard of and innovative? What if I could create the kind of life that would allow me to homeschool my son, bring my research to the community, and earn a living? But first, how would I take something as abstract as my English research and turn it into something other than an essay, dissertation, or class?

❊

I always encourage women entrepreneurs to become members of Doyenne. I love to tell them that all they need is the word "the" and that organization will help them build a sustainable business. I'm kind of joking, but not really.

By the time I had become a button-wearing member of this nonprofit for women entrepreneurs, I'd taken several business classes in the community. Neither the mentors nor instructors knew how to help me move my idea from a dissertation project to a business concept. But Amy, one of Doyenne's co-founders, did.

I'll never forget how she lit up and drew closer to me as I talked to her about my work. She pulled out her red journal, asked me questions, and got to writing. "What do you imagine for your business five years from now?" I answered. "What kind of  changes would you like for it to make in the world?" I answered. "What kind of activities do you see yourself doing?" I answered. "What kind of products would you make?" I answered. Before long, she had sketched out a full plan, a blueprint, for the business that would be known as Infamous Mothers. It started with the changes I wanted to make in the world. Somehow, in the form of a small startup, all of the seemingly unrelated parts of my life had come together. Nothing, not even the ugliness or pain, had been wasted. My life started to make sense. I began to make sense.

❖

Amy is teaching us about value propositions. In doing so, she is asking us to think about our "purple cow," the thing that sets us apart from everyone else, the thing that makes us the best at what we do. I'm thinking. These questions make me blush and feel uneasy. Deep down inside, I know the answer. But who am I to say it aloud? Who am I to own it? My purple cow is that I both have

the education and the personal experience that best qualifies me to create products and deliver services for the women we call Infamous Mothers.

Imagine that. Who would've thought that my biggest source of shame—my failed relationships and single parenting—would somehow be valuable?

V.

I'm at Panera Bread listening to a woman tell me her story. She's not a mother, but she has cared for and raised children, so she is a mother. Her tale includes stories about her imprisonment, her sister's molestation, her mother's untimely death. She tells me about another sister's battle with depression and her own struggle with survivor's remorse. Although hers is not included in this book, her story echoes all of ours. I fight back the tears. I tap my pen, shake my leg. I struggle to keep it all together. I allow myself to feel the fullness of her words, her wisdom; the raw, unprocessed hurt; the guilt; the need to make sense of it all. I bear these with her for my own accountability. She explains to me that she has earned her four-year degree. And, as if embarrassed, she shares that she wants to go back to school to become a therapist. I borrow her pen, pull out my notebook, become her scribe. This is the story of another Infamous Mother. Although our book has come to an end, her story reminds me that our work is just beginning. ❖

Infamous Mother Reflections...

Hazel Symonette, Ph.D.

Sagashus Levingston has richly blessed us with this inspiring "roots and wings" life lessons book. It illuminates and magnifies stories that nourish and unleash positive, provocative possibilities while short circuiting naysaying energies that shrink small.

I am feeling powerfully blessed and filled to overflowing with gratitude to have witnessed the birthing and nurturing of this exquisite book to full-term.

Reflecting on my Sistah friend's journey conjured up the revelation that I too am an infamous mother: a catalyzing, boundary-spanning transgressor who helps birth positive, provocative possibilities where there appear to be none... however cleverly disguised they might be!

I am a faithwalking social justice peace warrior with catalytic ancestral seeds planted deep in me. Committed to radical love, I strive to unleash lives—lifting and lighting futures for the greater good, in spite of whatever! I am a community mother without biological birthing experience—a midwifing soul mother who walks by insight and not simple sight. Mothering sooo many without asking permission and transgressing conventional legitimacy profiles and protocols, I am fueled by the power of things believed but not yet seen.

As radiant light bearers and light spreaders, we each can walk with this kind of *Appreciative Inquiry* stance fueled by a *Growth Mindset*. We scan and search for **sparks of positive, provocative possibilities**, remembering to track and fan and ignite even the smallest candles!

Mothering Spirits acknowledge and lovingly embrace the full spectrum. That generative touch determines whether one is stillborn after birth or fully born into the radiance of one's best self to do one's best learning, best engaging, best work for the greater good and one's own greater good.

How one mothers, nurtures, and guides depends on WHO one nurtures, and on what they and we have to responsively work with towards growth, readiness, and preparedness for what is yet to unfold.

All living beings have required mothering presence and mothering energies at some point in their life journey. The nature of that relational connection determines who and how one emerges and evolves from the dependence of infancy and childhood into full-term self-efficacy and sustainability.

One can be this kind of Infamous Mother at any age, stage, gender, or whatever intersectional identities. We must decenter self with empathic perspective taking, radical love, and arrogant humility in order to provide such Helpful-Help for the greater good, in spite of whatever.

Let's get busy! ❋

Your Privilege Will Not Protect You

[Sagashus Levingston delivered this speech at the Women's March in Madison, Wisconsin, on January 21, 2017. For many reasons, she improvised the final part in the live version. So it is not included here. But the final paragraph is its actual ending.]

Where and how do I enter this space? The expectation is for me to stand here and deliver a speech that highlights the ways in which white women failed this country on November 8, 2016. Some expect me to say, "While you, white women, were driving around with bumper stickers saying 'I'm with her,' 94 percent of black women and 63 percent of Latina women who voted were at the polls VOTING for her. Only 47 percent of you showed up." I am suppose to ask, "Where were the rest of you?" For some, the expectation is for me to tell you how much we don't trust you. How black and brown women are tired of cleaning up your messes just to be thrown out like trash and dismissed after the work has been done. Others want this speech to be about our refusal to form alliances with you until you apologize for historically putting your own needs and wants ahead of ours and other women's—and for your role in oppressing the marginalized. But to ask me to do this is to ask me to step out of character and to be someone I am not. There are far better women who are far more qualified to have that conversation with you and to give that speech. So today, right now, what I have to offer you is me. I show up as a woman in a space of women. I show up vulnerable.

Today, I am standing at the intersection of many identities: black, bald-headed, full-figured, single mother of six children, four different fathers, poor... PhD candidate, entrepreneur... woman. Which one shall I channel for this occasion? Which part of me is welcomed here? Who shall I evoke? Who shall I leave behind? And what will my choice cost me? Which one of me doesn't need health care, an equal and sustainable wage, clean air and water? To ask me to choose is a trick question. It's to vote against myself. It's to amputate parts of me in favor of an agenda that is not interested in all of me. That is unwise.

So, on this day, I make the choice to stand here: black, bald-headed, full-figured, single mother of six by four, poor... PhD candidate... entrepreneur... woman. And I give you all of me because it's all I have to give.

I tell you this very personal decision because any good feminist knows that the personal is ALWAYS political. That means you, like me, are standing here at the intersection of many identities—all shaped and influenced by race, class, sexuality, ability. Which parts do we amputate? Which feminists do we promote here today: whites, blacks, Latinas... Who do we leave behind—feminist men, Muslims, Asians, members of the LGBTQUIA community? And what will our choices cost us? Who here does not need health care, an equal and sustainable wage, clean air and water? Are these trick questions? To choose one identity over the other, will we in fact be voting against ourselves, against all women? Will we be amputating parts of a collective right to equality and justice, the right to overthrow oppression? And if so, we have to ask ourselves whose agenda are we serving if it isn't recognizing all of us? And is that wise?

I agree that the measure of a society is how it treats its women and girls. But I believe that one of the best measures of a society is how it treats those women and girls most marginalized—teen moms, women on drugs, sex workers, women and girls experiencing homelessness, impoverished women, single mothers, women in low-income housing, women on welfare, women of color, women with mental and physical health challenges, women experiencing domestic abuse... victims of rape.

I believe that a healthy society is one in which those at the center scream in agony when those furthest away are cut. It hurts when they hurt. It cries when they cry. And it moves and acts on their behalves. Equally and more importantly, it is invested in making sure

Copyright 2017 James Edward Mills

they have the tools and resources to act on their own behalves. And I believe this because I understand that most things—if not all things—in life are only as strong as its most vulnerable parts. And what I know, standing here at the intersection of so many identities, is that contrary to what we'd like to believe, at any given point pieces of us are always on the fringes. And if that's not the case now, it's only a matter of time. Your privilege will not always protect you. It will not keep your water clean or your mind sane or your body intact. It will not keep you from amputating parts of yourself to fit someone else's agenda.

So what do we do? Is this a trick question? To answer is to assume that I know what you're willing to give up for whatever needs to be done. It's to assume that your stakes in this are the same as my own. It is to assume that you understand that your fate is tied to mine and that this march is not just one big cathartic moment that ends as soon as we all drift away. And wouldn't all of that be presumptuous of me?

I want to tell you to read. Read wide and read deep about the oppression that now directly impacts you and the ones that have been impacting me. But will you? I want to tell you to put your dollars—with no strings attached—behind programs already doing the work like the YWCA, DAIS, the Catalyst Project, the Doyenne Group. But will you? I want to tell you to sponsor black businesses so that we can build up our communities and increase our chances of protecting ourselves in these uncertain times. But will you? I offer you no takeaways or no calls to action because I don't know enough about how far you will go when you are no longer in a sea of pussy hats. Instead, I leave you with a message as uncomfortable as the one I began with. More specifically, I leave you with a question: What exactly are YOU going to do after today? ✣

General Study Guide

1. In what ways have the stories in this book confirmed your biases about "infamous mothers?" How have they challenged them?

2. Find a story on the internet about an infamous mother. Read it. Now ask yourself, based on what I have read in *Infamous Mothers*, how can I approach this story in a new way?

3. In what ways are you similar to at least one mother in this book? In what ways are you different from her?

4. Which of these mothers would you like to have lunch with? Why?

5. Which story challenged you the most? Why?

6. Do race and class shape the circumstances of these women's lives? Why or why not?

7. Can you identify any challenges in these stories that speak to universal women's issues? If so, please list them.

8. How are the challenges you listed above shaped by race and class? (Note: Your answers may or may not overlap with responses to question six.)

9. Trauma is part of many of these women's lives. What trauma seems to be consistent in most of the stories?

10. Some of the women in this book pursue entrepreneurship. Why? How is their choice to become business owners consistent with or different from popular narratives about what it means to pursue business?

11. Choose a woman to study. Chart her path from challenge to triumph. Create a visual road map that demonstrates her journey.

12. If this book has inspired you to engage, recommit to, or continue working on one women's issue, what is it?